LANDMARKS

LANDMARKS

Reflections

on Anthropology

Andrew Strathern

The Kent State University Press

Kent, Ohio, and London, England

© 1993 by The Kent State University Press, Kent, Ohio 44242

All rights reserved

Library of Congress Catalog Card Number 92-32403

ISBN 0-87338-479-2

Manufactured in the United States of America

Library of Congress Cataloging-in-Publication Data

Strathern, Andrew.

Landmarks : reflections on anthropology / Andrew Strathern.

p.   cm.

Includes bibliographical references and index.

ISBN 0-87338-479-2

1. Ethnology.   2. Ethnology—Papua New Guinea.   3. Papua New Guinea—Social life and customs.   I. Title.

GN325.S76   1993

301—dc20   92-32403

∞

British Library Cataloging-in-Publication data are available.

Contents

Preface

The essays in this volume represent points of time, space, and perspective as these have appeared to me at crucial junctures in my life as an anthropologist. Although there is little in them that is explicitly autobiographical, they do nevertheless indicate landmarks, since most of them were delivered on occasions of public lectures when I was taking up, or newly exercising, a different role and status from ones I had occupied earlier. Most of my writings have been of a technical and ethnographic kind and have concentrated on the field areas where I have worked in the Highlands of Papua New Guinea since 1964. However, in these public addresses, often delivered to a majority of non-anthropologists, I was moved to consider matters in a more general way, while still drawing on inspiration from the field studies themselves. Inevitably, therefore, they reflect the ambience of their times and thus can be seen as constituting a kind of historical evidence of changes both in the subject at large and in my own thinking about it, a point also alluded to in Chapter 3.

The purpose in bringing these pieces together is threefold: first, to make them available either in a more accessible form than before or for the first time; second, to use them as a mirror for some trends in the discipline, including a number of unresolved issues which continue to challenge anthropologists; and third, to present them as a testing ground for such ideas as I have myself developed in the midst of a perhaps unprecedented flux of temporary "-isms" in anthropology, currently evident in an exaggerated version of the long-standing debate about anthropology as a science or as a humanistic study. In a sense, it is certainly the current phase of turmoil which has prompted me to look back over the years, not for the purpose of reflection only, but as a means of seeking out what may be enduring or what may indicate a decisive and important break with the past.

The papers are largely as they were composed, or delivered, but certain passages have been rewritten or omitted to aid in clarity of exposition, and a few later references have been added where most relevant. They still stand substantially as a historical record. The afterview considers the outcome of my "restudy" of the papers in more detail, but two matters can be signaled early on. First, what is most enduring and has changed least over time in my interests has been the concern with the relationship between the praxis of fieldwork and the production of anthropological theory. Second, what has changed most is the form of my actual theoretical ideas, as the stances that were current in the 1960s have been progressively modified and as I have reached, in a broad fashion, for fertile findings and concepts from other disciplines to help me solve problems arising out of my fieldwork. Fieldwork has been for me the still point of the turning world; but out of those turns, new perspectives ceaselessly emerge and call for recognition.

I am grateful to my wife, Gabriele Stürzenhofecker, for stimulating discussion on the papers included here, for providing me with some needed references and for her valuable comments on the entire manuscript; to Mrs. Patty Zogran for preparing and typing the manuscript in all of its drafts; to Thomas Mullane for reading the manuscript and suggesting some improvements; and to Joanna Hildebrand at Kent State University Press for her extremely helpful copy-editing work. My thanks also to the people of the field areas in Papua New Guinea where I have worked since 1964, for sharing their lives and their thoughts with me over the years.

LANDMARKS

ONE

Anthropology and the Study of

Social Change in Papua New Guinea

1974

A tremendous amount of anthropological research has been done in Papua New Guinea, and the results of that research, where properly done and published, form a record which is now a part of the country's general cultural heritage. That is good; but to have records is not enough, and it is not enough for the anthropologist simply to continue to make records. Our concern must be with problems of change and continuity in Papua New Guinea society, and we need to know what is actually happening now and why. To illustrate this starting point, I will recount two events that I saw in one part of the country at the end of 1973.

In the last week of December 1973 and the first week of January 1974, I was staying in the Mount Hagen area and observed two ceremonies. The first was the opening of a church in a new village to be occupied by mission converts. Neighboring expatriates from a tea research station and the Lutheran mission, together with an administration officer from the local government council, were all invited. There were prayers, speeches in the lingua franca *tok pisin*, and a European-style meal. The formal opening was followed during the next few days by an extensive killing of pigs and a distribution of pork to some thirty surrounding local groups and to evangelists and leaders within the mission. As soon as this celebration was over, many of the people, including the Member of the national parliament, the House of Assembly, moved on to take

The material for this chapter is based on my inaugural lecture as professor of Social Anthropology given at the University of Papua New Guinea in February 1974. It is reprinted with permission of the University of Papua New Guinea.

1

part in an event that might appear to be very different: a full traditional funeral for an important clan leader. Mourners smeared themselves with wet clay as a sign of their grief and made ceremonial charges around a dancing ground to show their potential aggression towards groups who might be suspected of having caused the death through sorcery. In one of his speeches the House of Assembly Member pointed out that his people had not performed a funeral ceremony of this kind for the last eighteen or twenty years, since it had earlier been forbidden by the incoming missionaries. It was therefore, he said, in a sense a new custom that they were just trying out. He took great pains to direct the movements of the mourners properly and to ensure that the displays of aggression did not go too far. After some days the mourning phase was completed with contributions of food and pigs from all the groups nearby and a pig-killing, after which legs of pork were presented to all those who had helped in mourning as a sign of goodwill toward neighboring political groups. The most elaborate day of mourning had been December 31, 1973, and the pig-killing took place in the first week of January 1974. The Member emphasized this turning point in time between the old and new year and said, "We used to think that after colonial control, when self-government came, our lives would be completely changed, but this is not so. We shall still cook pigs and we shall continue to eat our food as we did in the past."

Both of these events were thus "new" in certain respects. Living in a village area surrounding a Christian church is seen by people as a part of the "new" way of life introduced by outsiders. The funeral ceremony was new also, but differently so, for it was an innovation that drew its inspiration directly from the people's own past, their history, and thus might be said to represent clearly the "old" way. Both occasions also ended with a general distribution of pork as a show of good feeling toward neighbors and a means of renewing exchange relationships between the host group and others around it.

Events of this kind are not unusual in Mount Hagen nowadays. They form an important part of the people's adaptation to the total processes of change affecting them. In their mixture of new and old forms (where the term "new" has itself to be interpreted in more than one way), they constitute a microcosm of much more widely spread processes and events taking place throughout Papua New Guinea and reflected also in aspects of recent government policy. It is one of the most pressing, and to my mind interesting, tasks of the social anthropologist working in the country to observe, study, report, comment on, and, if he or she is employed at the University of Papua New Guinea (UPNG), teach about these emerging forms of adaptation from his or her own particular point of view. My aim is to expand on that proposition, and in the course of doing so, both to advance some criticisms of what we as anthropologists have been doing so far in Papua New Guinea and, incidentally, to defend some of the siblings in my tribe (and myself) against some other criticisms of us which have been made.

Since I am concerned with continuity and change, it seems appropriate at the beginning to refer to the inaugural lecture given by the Foundation Professor of Social Anthropology, Ralph N. H. Bulmer (now deceased) in 1969. In his lecture at UPNG, Professor Bulmer gave a very informative summary and discussion of the history of research work by social anthropologists within Papua New Guinea, elucidating both the importance of work done in the area for the development of social anthropology as a subject and the significance of anthropological work for on-going social problems in this country. What I want to stress is that it is important to be concerned as much with the latter as with the former, as much with the significance of anthropology for Papua New Guinea as with the significance of Papua New Guinea for anthropology. This does not mean that I am in any way suggesting the conversion of the whole of anthropology itself into an "applied" subject or that I am regarding it merely as a handmaiden available for use by agents of social change and economic development. Not at all. It does mean, however, that the anthropologist must be able to show the relevance of his or her subject and its findings to the contemporary situations from which our students are drawn, from the multitude of rural and urban communities across the country from Bougainville to the Irian Jaya border.

In his inaugural lecture of 1969, Professor Bulmer provided some interesting insight on problems that appeared even more

sharply five years later. While highlighting some of the achievements of anthropologists, for example in the field of ecological
studies he said,

> Anthropologists often point out that the geographical and cul-
> tural diversity of New Guinea not only provides a tremendous
> wealth of situations in which traditional forms of culture and so-
> ciety can be studied, but that this initial diversity, together with
> the very varied influences of European contact, provide a great
> laboratory for the study of social change. In fact, although a fair
> amount of relevant or potentially relevant factual information
> has been gathered, one cannot say that studies of social change
> in this country have yet contributed much of significance to the
> development of science. (1969:18)

Here again I would change Professor Bulmer's emphasis a little.
Can we say that these studies have contributed much, potentially
or actually, to the development of Papua New Guinea? Of course,
the development of science itself does matter, at least to some people, and in order to make his contribution a valid one the anthropologist must try to ensure that his findings are soundly based in
scientific method. Yet it is also worthwhile to stress the need to go
further than that, the need to connect the findings of our subject
with contemporary problems. In general, the better the anthropology we do, the better it will be able to contribute to development
in a true, human sense. I will come back to this proposition later.
In the meantime, let me look at the two disciplines of anthropology and sociology, much I hope as a participant observer-
cum-analyst from outside would do, in order to see to what extent
we are geared to fulfill the aim of studying and discussing emerging forms of adaptation.

Given that anthropology and sociology are disciplines frequently paired together in academic departments, rather as in the
double-barrel names given to some tribes in the Highlands, we
should look, as we do in a political study of tribes, first at the nature of the alliance between these two subjects, and also at the
question of whether in origins or current practice they are really
different from each other. There are differences, I think, and these

can perhaps be appreciated best through a discussion of the kinds of field methods we employ. Social anthropologists have tended to emphasize two aspects of field method: detailed observation of action from the outside and a real attempt to understand the subjective meaning of action through studying the ways in which people express themselves in their own language. To fulfill either of these two aims effectively it is necessary to spend considerable time in the field on a project, to learn, if one can, the language of the people, and to live with them in order to gain an understanding of them as individuals within their society. Hence we have the classic formula of the social anthropological fieldworker: varying degrees of participant observation sustained over some weeks, months, or years at a time.

The general aims of studying people in action and trying to grasp the meaning of their actions to themselves are, of course, not at all peculiar to anthropology. The first is really a requirement for any of the social sciences, since the initial material we all deal with is the actions of people, past and present. The second corresponds as much, say, to the sociological theories of Max Weber as to the ethnographic aims of Bronislaw Malinowski in studying the Trobriand people. The general theoretical basis of social anthropology is in fact largely the same as that of sociology.

In what way, then, is it useful in the present context to see the relationship between these two subjects? It is not that anthropology is concerned with exclusively rural and traditional situations while sociology is concerned only with urban problems and situations of change. Such a pair of dichotomies would immediately give a false picture of the actual situation of societies in Papua New Guinea, since there are very few simple "traditional" situations in a pure sense, and at the same time certain traditionally based forms of behavior operate very strongly even in developing urban contexts. It is rather a matter of division of labor in field methods. In terms of field studies it is necessary to recognize that useful and interesting results may be obtained by investigators working in complex situations from which they attempt to abstract certain features for analysis by means of techniques of interviewing and sampling. This is the essential core of many projects we are accustomed to call sociological. The sociologist's focus is often on a large and heterogeneous population, from which segments or cross-sections are selected as samples for study. Direct observation is not possible, so interview schedules are devised, with more than one investigator typically involved. From the study emerges a composite picture of a problem or facet of social life in the wider conglomerate population. Clearly such a technique has been developed largely within the context of urban situations, and it contrasts with the social anthropological technique of participant observation sketched earlier. But my point here is not designed to mark out differences in a rigid way; I would argue that these differing research techniques can be complementary rather than antithetical. For example, in an urban situation in Papua New Guinea, it is very helpful for an investigator to have some idea of the ethnic backgrounds and interrelationship patterns of the population he is surveying. Conversely, in a rural context, once the main patterns of a people's social life are established, it is feasible to construct sample survey schedules that can provide information on particular problems. So, if it is the sociologist who is going to look at some immediate, broad-scale problems, it is the anthropologist who can best provide the background and critical control for such an enterprise.

However, my ultimate belief in this regard is that efforts to demarcate too narrowly respective fields or competencies belonging to "sociology" or "anthropology" will prove to be false and unrewarding. The differences implied—that the sociologist and the anthropologist are two different persons—are by no means the only ones that have been put forward as distinguishing these two subjects; they are merely ones which I myself find more useful to bear in mind than others which I definitely reject—for example, the outmoded notion that anthropologists study "primitive" and sociologists "civilized" peoples. Still, however one conceptualizes the matter, there is no doubt that there are some differences between the sociological and the anthropological approaches; we hope, though, that our students will be able to see and combine these approaches as a result of our teaching, rather than favoring one and rejecting the other.

Social anthropology as it is taught in Papua New Guinea looks and is allied two ways: towards sociology and social work on the one hand and towards prehistory and linguistics on the other. The development of aims and courses in both of these segments has proceeded apace. Linguistics hived off in 1973 to become a part of the Department of Language, itself a product of expansion and fission in the Department of English. But there remains close cooperation with this new department in the construction of courses on sociolinguistics and on major languages of Papua New Guinea and on language, culture, and thought. The rapid development of a revised set of courses on prehistory has shown the rationality of maintaining strong links, if not divided affiliations, with the Department of History, an interesting process given the general intellectual debate that has flourished for the last fifteen years or so on the relationship between anthropology and history. A double rapprochement has taken place. While we social anthropologists have become more and more conscious of the need to incorporate historical perspectives into our studies—indeed, how otherwise can we even begin to discuss questions of social change?—historians at UPNG have become increasingly aware that to find out or write anything about the history of Papua New Guineans they must grasp the anthropological viewpoint. A lively beginning toward providing materials for joint discussion has been made in the history department's regularly produced journal, *Oral History*. (This journal was later transferred to the Institute of Papua New Guinea Studies.)

Perhaps I may mention here two further viewpoints. First, it is important to see continuities in Papua New Guinea history through to the present, and the division we make between history and prehistory, seen in these terms, is somewhat artificial. The special contribution that prehistory can make is to carry the picture of the development of cultures within Papua New Guinea further back in time than can be done either by using documentary records or by following up oral traditions. In a very real sense prehistorians have the opportunity to dig out some of the foundations for nationhood, and they may well show us that those foundations go deeper than we had thought (Allen 1972; Golson 1970). Second, a point on the relationship between anthropology and history. There is a need for critical discussion and debate on the meaning and contemporary significance of the wide body of materials we know as oral traditions. The goal of interdisciplinary discussion does not simply or necessarily mean the abandonment of particular disciplinary points of view, and I suspect that perhaps when the anthropologists and historians really get together there may occasionally be some sparks flying!

I have been explaining some of the side alliances made with other departments through prehistory and linguistics, and intellectually these links are a source of much potential challenge and interest. But I have by no means covered the whole field. There is much to say about possible relationships between anthropology and law, for example, or anthropology and economics or, and in some ways particularly, anthropology and medicine. But many of these possible links can be seen as growing, not just directly out of the central subjects of anthropology and sociology, but also out of the theories and findings of these subjects as they are embodied in the social-work side of the departmental program. A great deal of work and imagination is being put into the construction of courses on social welfare, social policy, and community development, and the social work courses are also designed to lead, where appropriate, to professional qualifications and a career in social work itself. Since the social worker may be posted anywhere in the country, in urban or rural situations, we have to ensure that our students do have, through a combination of anthropology and sociology courses, a strong background knowledge of Papua New Guinea societies and the problems they are currently facing. Courses on community development can be and should be integrated into other courses so that the general aim of understanding emerging forms of adaptation can in fact be realized. This point brings me back to the general question of the relationship between anthropology and development studies, which I regard as particularly crucial in Papua New Guinea.

One charge sometimes brought against anthropologists is that they are opposed to development. The charge takes various forms, from the assertion that anthropologists want people's customs to be preserved so that they can study them and implicitly gain profit for themselves in doing so (hence the "culture exploiter" image that has been propagated recently) to the idea that the anthropologist is some kind of anarchist whose views run counter to those of the official administrating power. Paradoxically, while a colonial government is in power the suspicion is likely to be that the anthropologist's presence is vaguely subversive; while in post-colonial times in countries other than Papua New Guinea anthropology itself has been labeled the child of colonialism, a subject which could flourish only under the aegis of colonial control.

The key to understanding these views is found in the nature of anthropological field technique on the one hand and the history of anthropological theory on the other. The standard anthropological field technique is that of participant observation. Participation can never be complete, but the aim is to live close to and associate with the people being studied. The result is that the anthropologist acquires a particular set of images. To the people being studied, the anthropologist may be quite popular as a result of the attempt to cross linguistic and cultural boundaries; to government officers, however, uneasy about the inflow of ideas into the area they control, the fieldworker's presence is a potential source of disturbance. In the past the anthropologist's behavior also would tend to be regarded as breaking caste rules, albeit in the name of a professional purpose. To a further set of outsiders, in turn, the anthropologist's "inside knowledge" of the people is likely to make him or her appear unjustifiably inquisitive, whereas in fact much of this knowledge comes through ordinary participation in conversations after a reasonable fluency in the language of the people studied has been acquired.

Second, the question of anthropology as a child of colonialism has been commented on by Adam Kuper, who writes:

It has been suggested that social anthropology flourished as a distinct specialty only because it was convenient in a colonial age to concentrate upon the study of "primitive people" and to separate them conceptually from other men. Now that this no longer has a political value, the social anthropologist is forced to recognize the unity of human societies and he will soon find that what he is doing is indistinguishable from sociology. (1973:232)

Kuper points out later that in post-colonial times the anthropologist enters a world "in which the politically dominant values are those of 'development' and 'modernization,' and he will be challenged to show that his work contributes to nation-building" (234).

The first argument here is interesting and undoubtedly has some truth, but it is oversimplified. There is no doubt that in the past anthropologists, like others, have been guilty of ethnocentric attitudes towards the people they have studied, but the whole purpose of modern social and cultural anthropology is to develop ways and means of overcoming such attitudes. Second, it is specifically anthropology, through its link with prehistory, that is especially concerned with the problem of the unity of human societies, and this problem can be usefully looked at only within the sort of evolutionary and comparative framework which can actually demonstrate to us that mankind is indeed one in many respects. And, third, to argue for the unity of human societies at one level in no way obliterates the fact that there are cultural differences between peoples, and we must take very seriously the study of these differences if we are to achieve intercultural communication and understanding, a task in which anthropological concepts and methods are of considerable value.

Despite this formal modification of Kuper's first argument, I am happy to agree with his second proposition, and I choose on this point, also, to add a comment on the kind of anthropological research currently being conducted in this country. The challenge is, as Kuper has put it, whether the anthropologist can show that the discipline is relevant to problems of development and nation-building. The answer is emphatically yes; moreover, each worker can and must show such relevance in his or her own particular way. It is true, however, that there are problems concerning the kinds of contributions the anthropologist can make or has been making.

The first problem is that there is a lag in research methodology from the times when some anthropologists were predominantly concerned with building mechanistic structural-functional models of the small-scale societies they studied in the field. Such a model would not deal with processes of change, but would tend to portray an equilibrium implying continuity and repetition. The problem of how to create models that will represent or take account of change has greatly challenged anthropologists in the last twenty years; yet to some—certainly not all—graduate students just beginning their research careers, that kind of functional model (and it is not the *only* kind of functional model) which shuts out aspects of social change still perhaps has attraction, leading to the second problem. A good deal of the elaborate field research carried out in Papua New Guinea is done by graduate students. Every anthropologist has to start somewhere, and a vast amount of excellent basic research is being carried out in this way. However, there is a potential drawback. For graduate students the field experience represents a kind of initiation into the mysteries of anthropological field method and ethnography-writing. Lacking in advance of arrival good up-to-date information on processes of social change and on where these are occurring, the student coming from another country sometimes decides that in order to be initiated properly he or she wants to work in an isolated area that has not been subject to significant changes. The search for a field area of this kind proceeds to the outer fringes of the Highlands area. While this has the excellent and valuable results of increasing ethnographic coverage, refining our analytical models, and, occasionally, of bringing to public notice the difficulties of isolated tribal peoples, it has also the unfortunate consequence of allowing important areas of research into problems of change to be ignored. Urban anthropology, for example, is as yet relatively undeveloped, while field anthropologists use the towns merely as bases from which to disappear into the rural areas. I have great sympathy with this practice, since that is what I do myself; I feel most at home in rural areas, especially since as a child I was brought up on a rural farm away from town. But perhaps one effect is that an incomplete image of what is occurring in Papua New Guinea society as a whole is maintained and propagated abroad as well.

Furthermore, the idea of the isolated society is, in its pure form, a myth. When the first explorers dropped into the Highlands area in the early 1930s, they were indeed moving into a society that had been isolated from the outside world. But that historical experience can only occur once. There may be good academic as well as emotional reasons why a research worker wishes to be freed from considering too many aspects of change. But there is always the danger that one may actually overlook the processes of change that have already occurred, for example, demographic changes caused by the introduction of new diseases, which of course can spread through populations otherwise unaffected by the presence of outsiders. Studies of such populations may tend to be predicated on the notion of a static society prior to European contact. Again, in its pure form, this is a myth, not a historically valid concept. For example, the work of prehistorians in various parts of Papua New Guinea is gradually revealing to us patterns of long-term change and development in the country's societies. In particular, the work done by Golson and others in the Highlands region indicates a long history of technological and ecological change in association with varying types of agriculture. So, although we do not have written records, archaeological work is beginning to show us that the notion of the precontact "zero point" of change is as false for Papua New Guinea as it was shown to be long ago for the African societies studied by anthropologists in the 1940s (see Riebe 1974, 1987).

The third reason for the relationship which has in the past held between anthropology and development studies is of a different kind from the first two. It is, frankly, that many anthropologists have disliked the kind of development policies pursued in Papua New Guinea in the past. In the journal *New Guinea*, arguments on the earlier five-year economic plan between Dr. Scarlett Epstein and others lucidly illustrated the conflicts of views involved at that time; while the present government's recently constructed eight-point plan, with its emphasis on rural development, self-reliance, and small-scale businesses based on distinctively Papua New Guinean forms of organization corresponds more closely to the intuitive feelings of anthropologists who have worked in particular villages and small communities throughout the country. The change here from a particular style of colonial development policy that emphasized large-scale foreign investment and speedy economic growth at the expense of local involvement to a policy that encourages local involvement and initiative even if the rate of overall growth is slowed down should encourage social anthropologists to discuss and evaluate the government's plan and make suggestions about the feasibility of actually implementing its various points.

In order to be true to a particular cultural and professional viewpoint, an anthropologist must, in commenting on development plans which emanate from the national centers of power, be continually mindful of the needs and aims of the local communities lived in and studied. Interests, values, situations, hopes— these are the things we have studied and about which we can talk with some claim to both accuracy and sympathy. An indigenous, rather than an expatriate, anthropologist could perhaps do so much better again. This does not necessarily mean that an anthropologist's views will be in conflict with central policy. Indeed, the present government plan does give recognition to desires for local identity and initiative as a specific part of wider national planning. National leaders are urging, for example, that Western ideas of law or business development must be regarded simply as experiments instead of being accepted as axiomatic and the only way to do things. If they do not fit Papua New Guinea's needs, they should not be clung to as if sacrosanct. There are enormous real difficulties, of course. If one sets about transforming a society in a particular direction, there are some very heavy entailments. But it should not be thought that people in Papua New Guinea have to change and become exactly like those in a Western or any other country.

That development plans should be directed towards improving the quality of life in definable and defensible ways and should correspond to the desires of people themselves may be taken as an initial axiom (Crocombe 1971). It should also be admitted, early on in discussion, that some conflicts between cultural values in the process of modernization are inevitable and that Papua New Guinean modes of organization may not be adapted to modern needs. In some cases, however, they *are* adapted, surprisingly so. What is more, it is a mistake to assume that indigenous modes of organization are themselves rigid or inflexible in the face of the demands of change.

The kinds of paradoxes and pitfalls for the student that exist in a context of change, such as holds in Papua New Guinea nowadays, are delineated well by sociologist Joseph R. Gusfield in a general discussion of the relationship between tradition and modernity in developing countries. Gusfield's purpose is to "call attention to the manifold variations in the relation between traditional forms and new institutions and values, variations whose possibilities are either denied or hidden by the polarity of the traditional-modern model of social change" (1971:15). Here we can draw a parallel between the traditional-modern dichotomy and the primitive-civilized one that Peter Worsley alleges has characterized the work of anthropologists in the past (Kuper 1973). If this has been so in the colonial past, then it is indeed a pity. What strikes me forcibly is that Gusfield's argument precisely corresponds to the modern view in social anthropology. In his article he lists a number of fallacies and explains why they are wrong. Each one of his points is worth considering and testing in the Papua New Guinea environment. Among the fallacies Gusfield identifies are: "developing societies have been (in the past) static societies"; "traditional culture is a consistent body of norms and values"; "old traditions are displaced by new changes"; "traditional and modern forms are always in conflict"; and "tradition and modernity are mutually exclusive systems" (1971: 17, 19, 21). Gusfield presents these as fallacies, rather than half-truths, in order to highlight his own position, which is derived largely from a study of the ethnography and history of India. His conclusion is that

> tradition is not something waiting out there, always over one's shoulder. It is rather plucked, created and shaped to present needs and aspirations in a given historical situation. Men refer to aspects of the past as tradition in grounding their present actions in some legitimating principle. In this fashion tradition becomes an ideology. . . ." (22)

In its essentials, Gusfield's article belongs to a tradition of writing in which the theory of unilinear social evolution and its offshoot social Darwinism is challenged and rebutted. This is a very vital point for a nation such as Papua New Guinea with its rich cultural and social background. It is in many ways the starting point for an enquiry into more specific equations and proposi-

tions. Which Papua New Guinean modes of organization/institu-
tions/values can in fact go hand in hand with or contribute to
which processes of political, economic, or social change? Are there
distinctive Melanesian solutions to business problems, and how
viable are these in the wider context of Papua New Guinea's economy? (cf. Latukefu 1972).

Within this field the internal predicament of populations has
been stated very clearly by Harold Brookfield. The starting point
for indigenous participants in a colonial economy is the fact of relative economic underdevelopment presented by the colonial
power as a facet of the indigenes' supposed general cultural underdevelopment. This notion of economic underdevelopment, true
though it is in certain technical ways, has become something of a
political myth, to be exploited by those countries that hold political
and economic power. People are now being told that they are "underdeveloped" much as before they were told that they were
"primitive." These peoples need initially to recover from that label
before they can effectively undertake their own further self-
development, holding the initiative truly in their own minds and
hands while doing so (see Denoon 1973). Given this sense of
underdevelopment, however, there is "a search for wealth," since
wealth is both a symbol of and a means to development, hence to
economic as well as political independence (Belshaw 1955). Immediately we should note that such a search is not an entirely new
cultural phenomenon. The search for wealth, as a means to a
blend of political and economic power, is intrinsic to most Papua
New Guinean societies, and was so well before European contact
became established there. So a drive for new forms of wealth may
well reflect established social values and may continue to do so for
a long time, unless the conflict between different forms of organization becomes overt and too difficult to handle other than by an
exclusive choice.

Full-scale studies which social anthropologists have in recent
years carried out on development problems and processes in particular local societies within Papua New Guinea include Richard
Salisbury's studies of the Siane and Tolai, the Epsteins' work on
the Tolai, Paula Brown's study of Chimbu, and Ben Finney's examination of entrepreneurship in Goroka (Brown 1972; A. L. Epstein

1969; T. S. Epstein 1968; Finney 1973; Salisbury 1962, 1971). Their findings need to be compared carefully with the Peter Lawrence's work on cargo cults, for Lawrence stresses and documents carefully the epistemological basis of economic activity in Madang society (Lawrence 1964, 1968). We need many more studies of this kind, but those we have already give us at least an initial framework from which we can try to extrapolate and predict further processes of change. The important thing is to note that political and economic change are linked. One of Salisbury's main points, for example, is that Tolai entrepreneurship was never divorced from political leadership; the entrepreneur was always a local political leader. What is more, he was a leader who appealed to supporters in "traditional"—that is, indigenous rather than foreign—political idioms. Hence, Tolai society in the period since European contact has been characterized both by economic dynamism and by a proud adherence to aspects of Tolai tradition and culture (cf. Crocombe 1972). The same mixture can be seen in the Mataungan Association itself. Gorokan economic history shows the same pattern too: the entrepreneur succeeds, at least initially, because he is a group leader and at the same time because his strength within the group is largely self-made, albeit based on very definite community support. Finney goes so far as to argue that Gorokan society was actually "preadapted" by its traditional values to the introduced capitalist economy and thus threw up entrepreneurs almost as soon as opportunities presented themselves. Gorokan "tradition" thus becomes in his treatment rather like a version of the capitalist ethic, as does Tolai tradition in the picture given by Scarlett Epstein.

Finney perhaps goes too far here. Gorokan wealth was not traditionally put to the same social and political uses as is wealth in a Western capitalist industrial system, and we should not imagine that his study demonstrates any kind of automatic and replicable conversion process from indigenous to imported economic systems. Nevertheless his work does show some of the potentialities of anthropological method for the study of economic change, whether we agree with his substantive interpretations or not. What we need is similar work on a number of societies, which would help to give us reliable pointers, and, in depth, on the extent, pace, and implications of economic change. There is, again, a similar need for work on emerging political problems and on the whole question of the creation of a class society and elitism in Papua New Guinea (see Standish 1973). This would not be "research for the sake of research." Paradoxically, if it were, one might argue against it, as I once heard it argued in a seminar by a very able Papua New Guinean, suggesting that research is not needed because "it has all been investigated before in Africa and you can read about it in the books." But Africa is not Papua New Guinea. There are similarities and differences. We urgently need studies that will keep abreast of and inform us on social changes so that we know in what directions Papua New Guinea society is going and how to suggest policies to move it in directions that the people and the government desire.

Another implication of the work of both Salisbury and Finney is one which bolsters Gusfield's statement that "tradition becomes an ideology." Ronald Crocombe, in his enquiry into the nature of Pacific cultures, notes that "one of the real needs is to transfer at least some of the respect attached to earlier forms of authority . . . to the new forms. Otherwise there is a danger that although respect for other forms of authority diminishes, the new forms are not treated with any respect. This may result in those in power using crude force to get obedience" (Crocombe 1972:11–12). It is very difficult to create respect of this kind entirely in modern terms. The Tolai leader has always appealed to established norms and idioms as well as insisting on the need for forms of economic innovation. Finney also stresses how in the 1960s, at any rate, the most successful Gorokan entrepreneurs strove to be regarded as generous "big-men," for on this image much of their basic credit depended. Respect for authority is essentially based on some kind of projection of the parental image, and in a historical context such as exists in Papua New Guinea that must mean a traditionally valid image of some kind. For this reason the publication in the *Papua New Guinea Post-Courier* newspaper of a picture of the Chief Minister, Michael Somare, in the full regalia of his office as an initiated leader within his clan in his own local area, was a most interesting event (*Post-Courier*, Jan. 8, 1974). I at once showed this picture to a number of Hageners staying with me, and on seeing the shell

decorations they commented, "Oh, he must be a big-man, then."
The visual symbol of shell wealth had registered with them immediately in a way that even the verbal title of "Chief Minister" could
not possibly do. In becoming initiated in this way, the Chief Minister was undoubtedly involving himself in a statement of the
worth of tradition—not just in the past but in the present as well—
in exactly the same way as were the Hagen people I was watching
in the first week of 1974 during the revival of their funeral custom.

I have tried briefly to sketch some ways in which anthropological viewpoints and studies have so far contributed to understanding change in Papua New Guinea. A tremendous amount more
needs to be done. Although I would not envisage the disappear-
ance of social anthropology entirely into a branch of development
studies, I do think that Cochrane has made an interesting proposition in suggesting that there be at least a branch of social anthropology known as development anthropology to replace the old
title of applied anthropology in a post-colonial context. That is,
there should be both an anthropological attitude towards development in general and a body of anthropological ethnography on actual cases of change, leading to implications for policy decisions.
Not all change involves what we speak of usually as economic or
other forms of development, of course, and there is a need to set
studies of development into the wider context of studies of change
in general.

Finally, I cannot resist making a plea and expressing a hope.
While it is not a major purpose of courses in our department to
produce large numbers of sociological and anthropological research workers, it is legitimate to hope that we shall produce
some, at least, who will find their own identity and ways of doing
things in the subject and who will be able to take on positions both
within the university itself and allied bodies such as the National
Museum and the Institute of Papua New Guinea Studies and
within the general body of the country's public service. If there is
something in social anthropology that is worthwhile for Papua
New Guinea, it is worthwhile pushing as hard as possible for the
subject to be "localized"—taken over, reinterpreted, reshaped,
and reapplied by Papua New Guineans themselves. The new institute is going perhaps to be a crucial factor in this respect, and I

do hope very much that, like the museum, it will provide positions for young, indigenous, newly qualified social anthropologists to do research work. There has been for some time a feeling that too much of the research in the country is done by people from outside, as well as an impression that too many of the results do not effectively get back to Papua New Guinea. The university can provide the training for indigenous workers to overcome part of this situation, while it will be up to the government to determine whether there will in fact be career opportunities for such research workers, as I hope there will.

The hopes expressed in this lecture have at least partially been fulfilled today in the achievements of Dr. Wari Iamo, who is now director of the National Research Institute in Port Moresby, holding a Ph.D in Anthropology from the University of California, Berkeley; and of Dr. Jacob Simet, director of the Cultural Studies Division in the NRI, with a Ph.D on the Tolai people gained from the Australian National University. Both of these were students who worked with me in the 1970s.

References

Allen, Jim
    1970   The First Decade of New Guinea Archaeology. *Antiquity* 46:180–190.
Belshaw, Cyril S.
    1955   *In Search of Wealth.* American Anthropological Association Memoir No. 80. American Anthropological Association, Washington, D.C.
Brookfield, Harold
    1972   *Colonialism, Development and Independence: The Case of the Melanesian Islands in the South Pacific.* Cambridge University Press, Cambridge.
Brown, Paula
    1972   *The Chimbu.* Schenkman, Cambridge, Mass.
Bulmer, Ralph N. H.
    1969   Cultural Diversity and National Unity. Inaugural lecture. University of Papua New Guinea, Port Moresby.

Cochrane, Glynn

1971   *Development Anthropology.* Oxford University Press, Oxford.

Crocombe, Ronald

1971   Review of *Koro,* by Raymond F. Watters. *Journal of the Polynesian Society* 80(4):505–520.

1972   Preserving Which Tradition? The Future of Pacific Cultures. *Pacific Perspective* 1:4–15.

Denoon, Donald J. N.

1973   People's History. Inaugural lecture. University of Papua New Guinea, Port Moresby.

Epstein, Alfred L.

1969   *Matupit.* Australian National University Press, Canberra.

Epstein, Trude Scarlett

1968   *Capitalism, Primitive and Modern.* Australian National University Press, Canberra.

Finney, Ben

1973   *Big-Men and Business.* Australian National University Press, Canberra.

Golson, Jack

1970   Towards a New Guinea Nationhood. *Search* 1(5):192–196.

Gusfield, Joseph R.

1971   Tradition and Modernity: Misplaced Polarities in the Study of Social Change. In *Political Development and Social Change,* edited by Jason L. Finkle and Richard W. Gable, pp. 15–26. University of Chicago Press, Chicago.

Kuper, Adam

1973   *Anthropologists and Anthropology.* Allen Lane, London.

Latukefu, Sione

1972   The Place of Tradition in Modernization: An Islander's View. *Journal of the Papua and New Guinea Society* 6(2):3–11.

Lawrence, Peter

1964   *Road Belong Cargo.* Manchester University Press, Manchester.

1968   *Daughter of Time.* University of Queensland Press, St. Lucia.

Ogan, Eugene

1972   *Business and Cargo.* New Guinea Research Bulletin No. 44. New Guinea Research Unit, Port Moresby.

Riebe, Inge

1974   ". . . and then we killed": An Attempt to Understand the Fighting History of Upper Kaironk Valley Kalam from 1914–1962. Masters thesis, Department of Anthropology, Sydney University, Sydney.

1987   Kalam Witchcraft: A Historical Perspective. In *Sorcerer and Witch in Melanesia*, edited by M. Stephen, pp. 211–248. Rutgers University Press, New Brunswick.

Salisbury, Richard F.

1962   *From Stone to Steel*. Melbourne University Press, Melbourne.

Standish, William

1973   The Highlands. *New Guinea* 8(3):4–30.

TWO

Anthropology as Self-Analysis:

Some Reflections

1980

Anthropology is frequently associated in the mind of the public with the exotic, the primitive, and with skulls, particularly old ones. While the first and third of these have their proper place in the subject, and the second is in fact better regarded as a distorted image of the first and therefore to be subsumed in it, there are many other aspects too, and it is to these that I wish to draw attention. The task can be carried out in two ways, each involving a reciprocal reversal of perspective: by seeing the exotic in the light of what is familiar, and by seeing the familiar as, *per contra*, exotic or strange.

What is "exotic"? By definition, it is what is outside of our own experience, what we have not known before, and what, when we do know it, still appears difficult to understand. How then do we attempt to come to grips with the exotic? The only method is to proceed from the known to the unknown and in doing so use concepts and categories available to us from our existing knowledge and thought, itself firmly located in a particular cultural matrix. Yet in so far as our thought is located in such a matrix, it may be precisely this which keeps us from comprehending the unknown. We can hardly hope, however, to proceed from nothing to the unknown, leaping instantly into knowledge of it while throwing off all our prior concepts in one grand gesture. But my remarks so far

The material for this chapter is based on a Munro Lecture delivered at St. Andrew's University, Scotland, in February 1980. It was subsequently revised and published in 1982 in *Bikmaus* (Institute of Papua New Guinea Studies, Port Moresby) 3(3):93–105. The version printed here is closer to the text of the original lecture. Reprinted with permission of *Bikmaus*, IPNGS.

presume that the phenomenon is entirely inaccessible to preexisting knowledge, and this is incorrect. If the exotic is in fact partly familiar, it is the image of it as different that now blocks our understanding, and we must persuasively relate it to the familiar. In doing so, we may be able also to see aspects of the familiar that are in need of explanation. For, in turn, the definition of the familiar is that which we know so well in practice that we take it for granted and do not analyze it, and therefore, we may not adequately understand it at all—a point which Marxist exponents of the subject have labeled "misrecognition," seeing it as a result of ideology imposed on people by the dominant classes. This certainly happens, but the point can be made more widely that that which is so familiar to us that we see it as "natural," not in need of explanation, is precisely that which we need in fact to explain if we wish to understand our own social and cultural systems, and this can only be done by forcing ourselves to see these as, in this sense, exotic (see Hsu 1973).

The reciprocity of perspective is now clear, though it is still hard to see how to set in hand the task of achieving such a perspective. Logically, it can be done only from the familiar outwards, before attempting a return. That is how anthropology begins—with "other cultures," or at least with "other" aspects of a culture already known in part. When the return is eventually made, though, we may also begin to see how the initial analysis was influenced by unwarranted, if not ethnocentric, assumptions, and this will take us back to the data or the field for a fresh look, since all data are partly influenced by the observer's outlook.

This may begin to sound like an awkward furrow to plough (especially in a circle) or, similarly, an endless treadmill. Indeed it is, but there is nothing very arcane about it. All the problems I have sketched can be illustrated from the study of a topic familiar to everyone's experience—that is, kinship. To nonanthropologists it might be rather surprising to hear that anthropologists have struggled to formulate a universal definition of kinship and are still in disagreement. Two very distinguished scholars who have spent much of their professional lifetime on the problem, Rodney Needham and David Schneider, have made their separate declarations on it:

What information is given, then, by the report that an institution has to do with "kinship"? Nothing really about social facts. For the label designates no distinct type of phenomena; it provides no clue to comprehension; and it does not indicate the kind of analysis that will be appropriate. . . . To put it very bluntly then, there is no such thing as kinship, and it follows that there can be no such thing as kinship theory. (Needham 1971:4–5)

Biological facts, the biological prerequisites for human existence, exist and remain. . . . They are facts of life and facts of nature. There is also a system of constructs in American culture about those biological facts. . . . But these same cultural constructs have another quality . . . a symbolic quality, which means that they represent something other than what they are. . . . They serve in this respect as symbols precisely because there is no necessary or intrinsic relationship between them and what they symbolize. . . . They symbolize diffuse, enduring solidarity. . . . They symbolize trust. . . . They stand for the fact that birth survives death, and that solidarity *is* enduring. (Schneider 1968:116)

It is apparent here that Schneider's view is rather more productive and profound (in my selective quotation) than Needham's sharp logic-chopping. But they share a basic viewpoint, that words such as "kinship" cannot be given a standard cross-cultural meaning because to do so may violate the principles of logic in a given culture (Bloch 1977; Bourdillon 1978; Hanson 1979; Salmon 1978). Very similar debates have raged about the meanings of related sets of terms such as "marriage" and "descent," which have a particular resonance in Western usage. Thus Leach points out that a "minimal" definition of marriage will still not necessarily do for cross-cultural analysis, and that instead marriage is "a bundle of rights" (1961:105), and the pieces in the bundle may vary considerably. As to "descent," its definitions are legion, and so are the divergent views, predictably, of those who argue that it is or is not important in the social structure of the New Guinea Highlands societies, where my fieldwork has been done.

This might again appear an unpleasant morass into which the anthropologist is bound to sink more and more deeply as he or she reaches out to understand those "other cultures." But in fact this is not so; those feet are digging channels which let the water flow out and some bits of dry land appear. To say that we do not know *in general* what kinship is can help us positively to identify particular features of a culture while retaining the terms as a rough rubric or "odd-job" word, as Needham calls it, following his latter-day hero, Wittgenstein. To identify marriage as a "bundle of rights" encourages us to enumerate what the pieces of the bundle can be and how they cohere in different permutations. And to see how the concept of descent is variably deployed reveals to us that concepts are often embedded in "whole-system" typologies, and that such typologies influence deeply what we expect to find in a particular society. The overall message is that as means of classifying societies these broad terms have limited use; they need to be broken down further into their elements (Needham 1974:47).

Curiously enough, Needham's round assertion that there is no such thing as kinship (which taken literally, as a statement in an English sentence, is wrong, because the word certainly does have a set of meanings and referents in English culture) finds a set of allies in quite a different camp—that of Marxist analysts, for whom the term is ideological and therefore cannot be analytical. Indeed, in the strict usage of some Marxist scholars, perhaps all cultural units are to be seen as ideological and may never be elevated to the rank of explanatory principles, a status reserved for such gods in the machine as the class struggle and the relations of exploitation (Rey 1979:53; Thompson 1978:193–397). Marxist writers propose instead that the structural concept of the mode of production, with infrastructure divided into forces and relations of production and superstructure encompassing all else, is the only worthwhile tool of analysis. Let me turn then, to the merits and difficulties of this approach, since they illustrate my basic proposition even more forcibly than I have so far indicated with the example of kinship itself.

Marx's work on pre-capitalist societies was brief, fragmentary, and peripheral to his major analysis of capitalism. A recent and sensitive reexamination of this body of his writings seeks, notably, to refute the idea that Marx espoused techno-economic determinism with regard to the societies outside of the historical nexus of capitalism (Llobera 1979; Habermas 1979:142–146; Cohen 1978; Dumont 1977). The "project" of Marxist anthropology, however, has been, in the words of the editors of *Critique of Anthropology* (Summer 1979:235),

> an attempt to "annex" the realm of pre-capitalist societies to historical materialism; in other words to try to discover the . . . "determination in the last instance by the economy" in the examination of pre-capitalist societies. The project envisages these societies either as autonomous entities or as part of the world capitalist system.

This passage reveals a dilemma. Historical materialism itself is certainly in part an ideology, and might therefore fall foul of its own stricture that ideologies cannot explain social facts but can only be used to justify (or in this case attack) them. The editors themselves are uncomfortably aware that there is a political as well as a theoretical arm of the movement, and "is there not the risk as the result of the extensive borrowing from anthropology, that the Marxist project is neutralized?" (236; cf. Lienhardt 1964: 6–10; Salamone 1979). A point well taken and a fear justifiably expressed. The risk is, indeed, that the difficulty of combining the theoretical and political approaches may become too obvious, and if a disjunction develops—what? Presumably a failure of political resolve. If so, the editors' stance indicates a preference for the primacy of political, or moral, action over theory. But this is surely an unacceptable academic position. Yet why should Marx's theories have to apply to all those societies about which very little, comparatively speaking, was known in accurate detail at the time he wrote? For those with an empirical turn of mind this would appear an absurd position to start from. Why give oneself that handicap? But this would be to miss the point. If Marx was theoretically correct, then the practice he advocated would be scientific as well as morally right, and therefore unassailable. And if he was correct, his pronouncements should be correct about all cases, not just about capitalism, for otherwise the context of his vision might begin to shrink to the size of industrial Britain in the nineteenth century. Hence, the urgency of showing that he was right, either for pre-capitalist societies in themselves or for those societies as influenced from early on by the "world system" of Western capitalism itself.

I do not myself see the necessity of taking the Marxist project in this way. There is no reason why its hypotheses should have analytical privilege, though I would agree that as a voice of social conscience applied to specific cases, its power is considerable, hence its appeal to many people as thinking persons rather than academics and its ability to serve as a banner for those who seek radical changes in the structures of Western societies themselves. But it appears an act of desperate "imperialism" to wish to "annex" pre-capitalist societies entirely to subjugation within a theory designed primarily to handle other problems, and to justify such an annexation ultimately on ideological grounds. It would in fact mean that Marxist anthropology, for all its brilliant insights, is basically guilty of ethnocentrism just as much as the "colonial" or "bourgeois" anthropology its advocates have so bitterly, and with varying justification, attacked. We would, therefore, be back at square one, interpreting the unknown by the known and asserting that "laws" derived from the study of capitalism should apply universally, or that whenever capitalism has touched a society it at once becomes the determinant of factors within the society because it affects the economic base which determines all else. Every one of these points should be taken simply as a provisional hypothesis, for if not then the analysis can in principle be no better than those early analyses associated with Alfred R. Radcliffe-Brown that suggested the opposite picture of integration and stability. As practical hypotheses, however, and pointers to research, Marxist ideas are indeed of value: it is simply the case that they do identify important basic processes of change and conflict occurring throughout underdeveloped societies today. My restriction on this is just to add that they cannot be taken in a totalitarian way as assumptions. If Marxist analysis really requires us to be critical and reflective, it surely means that we have to identify our own historical position and, I would add, to avoid the kind of vitriolic rhetoric with which one doyen, André Gunder Frank, attacks another, Maurice Freedman (1979:201–212). Gunder Frank's hatred and wholesale condemnation, together with the claim that all anthropology is just ideology (unlike his Marxism, which is presumably both science and revelation), could lead to equally embittered counter-protests that states set up in the name of Marxism have not been free of domination and terror either. But to do so would be truly to sink in that morass I promised earlier we would trudge through.

What I am arguing is that the anthropological enterprise requires a remarkable feat of self-conscious intellect. To understand another society or culture we have, in a sense, to understand ourselves and our culture first; then, having that understanding, to suspend it and reach a different understanding of the society to be observed and analyzed. It is obvious that such a suspension is impossible. It is clear also that this formulation also suffers somewhat from what has been described as the "natural science model," the idea of the observer coolly looking down his microscope, emotionally uninvolved with his "object" of observation, and, by implication, also setting up a scientific series of facts as data and doing so in a value-free fashion. Again, a moment's reflection indicates that this is profoundly untrue of the process of social enquiry to which anthropology belongs (cf. Schutz 1970). The ideal I offer is one which can only be *post hoc*. In practice one goes into an enquiry with ideas and prejudices and comes out similarly laden, but with a rather altered set and a good deal more to sift through. The impossible, then, is not a prescription *at all* for the way in which fieldwork has to be done, but it is an ideal that we have to think about whenever we *represent* the society by writing about it. Perhaps it is in realization of this that some Marxist anthropologists, wary also of naive self-identifications with anything vaguely romantic or exotic, are suspicious of fieldwork itself. It is less problematic, perhaps, to deal with documents, "interrogating" them safely at a desk where they can't bite back. That is a viewpoint which, starting from a laudable self-realization, ends in a form of cowardice.

In fact, the meaning of anthropology is all contained within the loose prescription to practice participant observation, an activity that must be chameleon-like in its changes, but in every case requires the effort of human engagement with other persons; without that, we can never be shocked into further self-knowledge that will penetrate deeply enough to modify our views. The practice of participation will not necessarily have that result, of course. One can play roles. But one can also experience. Students in London sometimes ask me, "Did you cry at funerals to act out the role?" In practice, as all fieldworkers know, emotions are usually experienced very intensively in the field. Hagen people say that the Lutheran Mission has taught them not to cry too much or for long at a death and to do so inside the house, not in the open. For a while, they followed this; but many have now gone back to the large, public expressions of tears, songs, and speeches that form indigenous practices; and I found this, in fact, more congenial than the reverse (cf. Scheff 1977:484).

So, how do we move back from the exploration of other cultures into our own? Or, if fieldwork is done within the general ambit of one's own culture, what anthropological ideas, distilled from the work of others, can successfully be deployed? The most effective approach has been to use the ideas emerging from the work of symbolic anthropologists, and, where necessary, recognizing the forces of the Marxist paradigm.

One practitioner of this approach is Roy Wagner, a social anthropologist who has worked extensively among the Daribi people of Papua New Guinea. He has also written a book in which he outlines a basic theory of culture that he applies primarily to his own American society. Wagner starts from a view that "man invents his own realities," and he points out that fieldwork in social anthropology is a means of realizing the force of this truism through the pain and the humor of learning not just to observe but to practice. Anthropologists and the people they study are likely to experience a reciprocal "culture shock" in this process. Their questions to each other will reveal the inevitable naivete and touches of insight also. Wagner records a Daribi question put to him: "Can you anthropologists intermarry with the government and the missionaries?" (1975:19). The closed, segmental circuits of Daribi social life in colonial circumstances stand out by implication from the enquiry, which taken literally is to be answered simply as "yes." It also reflects another reciprocity: anthropologists are always asking people whom they can marry so the Daribi were repaying the compliment. The terms "native" and "anthropologist" become interchangeable. "Since plausibility is a function of the researcher's viewpoint, the 'culture' that he imagines for the native is bound to bear a distinct relation to that which he claims for himself" (Wagner 1975:26). In Wagner's case his interest clearly lies in symbolic forms, and he applies this to good effect in the analysis of advertising, a theme taken up also by Ronald and Catherine Berndt in their book dealing with Australian culture, *The Barbarians* (1973). For the anthropologist, advertising is simply a variety of magic, and as Richard Shweder has shown, Westerners are prone to magical thought in the sphere of personality judgments, a variable much manipulated in advertising practices. Shweder points out that we draw the conclusions we feel inclined to from evidence, though not those conclusions we are logically compelled to and certainly not those belonging to a different worldview. If a child organizes games, the mother or a neighbor draws the conclusion that he is self-confident, even though this may be an overgeneralization and to deny it would not be self-contradictory. An advertisement can play on such an association by depicting such a "self-confident" child organizing games and eating or wearing Brand Y. If the mother of a child who consistently organized games in the playground were to apologize for him and say that his father's ghost was in the playground and sometimes possesses him, she would be thought strange. If she declared his behavior was due to extensive conditioning from 18 months old, she would be asked, "Are you really his mother? Or are you some kind of . . . uh . . . scientist?" (Shweder 1977:640–641). Such responses break up the "normal" inferences people make and therefore require the reclassification of those who make them; to the contrary, advertising depends on the strong reinforcement of symbolic (and arbitrary) associations. Wagner's points link in here. "Advertising operates as a kind of 'inverse' or 'backwards' technology; it uses the intended effects of a product on people's lives, and human reactions to those effects, to build a meaningful identity for the product" (1975:62).

The process of communication is exactly analogous to that in magic, where intended effects are acted out in advance or signed on objects representing the person to be affected. Wagner instances the Daribi gardener's practice of reciting a spell as he piles up brushwood in his garden, identifying his hands with the claws of a bush fowl, "a bird that characteristically rakes forest debris into huge mounds to provide heat for the incubation of its eggs" (1975:63). Exaggeration and intensification are present in this image, just as in advertising, when a tire for a family car is associated with ones used on racing vehicles. Something of the excitement and "performance" of racing is supposed to be felt by the family-car driver when he uses that brand of tire, although there is no need for him to don a crash helmet or take corners on two wheels "anymore than a Daribi gardener finds it necessary to hop about and squawk like a bush fowl" (64). The objects themselves "inflate" life, since they are "mass-produced, completely replaceable," and "virtually as communicable and conventionalized as words: others know exactly what you have bought, probably know why you have bought it, and can get one just like it" (65). The Berndts make some parallel observations, citing the "humanization" of objects such as cars, perhaps leading a naive observer to suppose that Westerners had an animistic theory of machines: the ad "Cars love Shell" invites you to pour Shell gasoline into your car and so satisfy its desires—how very masculine (1973:144).

Another example of symbolic anthropology is Mary Douglas's book, written with economist Baron Isherwood, on "the world of goods." Rightly, Douglas points out that we need a theory of consumption as well as of production, and that economists' theories on consumption have lacked cultural awareness. Keynes, for example, treated saving as a result of a constant propensity to consume less than one earns. But why should such a propensity be constant? It will have its own parameters, which will vary. Similarly, why do people want goods at all? Economists answer that it is for subsistence, for welfare, and for display in competition with others. Not bad; but to work out the lineaments of welfare and the dimensions of display, attention to the function of goods in social communication as cultural markers is required. Douglas also attacks the distinction between subsistence and display that is used by economists as though they were perhaps real phenomena in the motivations of individuals. She points out that this is doubtful because subsistence goods also are cultural markers, and the whole distinction between luxury goods and others is false too. "Let us put an end to the widespread and misleading distinction between goods that sustain life and health and others that service the mind and heart—spiritual goods. That false distinction leaves a mass of unnecessary luxuries to be accounted for by a mixture of consumer gullibility and sinister advertising" (Douglas and Isherwood 1979:72).

Analytically, the distinction is false; ideologically, however, it does suit well the purpose of advertising. The whole distinction between subsistence and surplus is also one that is specifically a part of the industrial capitalist economy, and its power to influence the symbols we obey is thereby impressively demonstrated, even as its perniciousness in analysis is equally made clear. The same distinction led to vast debates in economic anthropology as to whether the economy has a surplus or not. It is even intertwined in Marx's own theories, for which a necessary point of departure is the idea of the production of a surplus beyond the actual or immediate subsistence needs of the direct producer. This surplus is then seen as appropriated by others in precapitalist formations, and in the capitalist formation it is imaged in the notion of surplus value.

Douglas points out that even in the choice of tools to do a job cultural statements are made and individual preferences are shown. She cites an example from Roland Barthes, the semiologist, of Brillat-Savarin, who liked coffee beans pounded by a pestle rather than ground to impersonal dust by an electric grinder. The pestle meant manual work, art, bodily skills, experience. Out of the mortar comes not dust but "a gritty powder, pointing straight to the ancient love of alchemy and its potent brews. The choice between pounding and grinding is thus . . . metaphysical. Market researchers know this hidden area well enough" (Douglas and Isherwood 1979:74). This sphere of experience is indeed highly exploited in an urban, industrial society where people still identify what is natural with what is "best" and with "the old times."

Another well-known anthropologist has made a brilliant contribution to this theme. Marshall Sahlins, in his book *Culture and Practical Reason* (1976), points out that Marx's idea of the use-value of products based on the proposition that they satisfy biological wants is curiously similar to that of Malinowski, who claimed no inspiration from Marx. But culture and history, with their specificity and their system, cannot be pitched out (1976:149–153). Sahlins goes on to show that Marx spoke of "impulses" and "wants" in consumption but that they are very general. Putting it this way enables Marx to shift these two categories from a relationship of mutual interdependence into one of hierarchy, so that consumption is subordinated to production, the latter alone having specificity of form through the definite sequential acts of the labor process (155). This aspect of Marx's thinking is what leads to "productionism" and is what has been criticized strongly by Habermas (160). Essentially, Mary Douglas is building on these same insights in her insistence that consumption be considered in all its cultural meaningfulness and specificity. That goods can act in a pure sense as cultural markers, which still have a deep social significance, is shown exactly by those goods in tribal economies that are symbolic counters of life itself—pigs and pearl shells in Mount Hagen—or of prestige itself, as are *kula* valuables in the Trobriands. Sahlins takes this insight back into Western society again in his chapter on *La pensée bourgeoise*, a play on Lévi-Strauss's famous *pensée sauvage*. One of his excursions is into edibility, a topic beloved also of Mary Douglas and Leach. What is meat? First, meat is an essential, central ingredient on plates of everyday food, peripherally supported by carbohydrates and vegetables: meat, potatoes, and two vegetables with gravy. Meat is a symbol of masculine strength (this point is exactly the same as that made for the Daribi by Wagner, an American anthropologist), and Sahlins suggests that this goes back to the Indo-European identification of cattle with virility. Meat is therefore a part of our basic diet: "hence also a corresponding structure of agricultural production of feed grains, and in turn a specific articulation to world markets — all of which would change overnight if we ate dogs" (Sahlins 1976:171). Plains Indians, who do eat dogs, would consider it odd how Americans let the animals roam at large and do not molest them, as compared with cows in India, at which Westerners express surprise, and some, like Marvin Harris, determinedly work to establish that techno-economic rationality does rule. Dogs and horses are not eaten because they participate as subjects in human society. Dogs are closely integrated into the family: a recent newspaper article in the *Guardian* indicated that they are becoming an awkward factor in divorce settlements, since their custody has to be decided. "Edibility, therefore, is inversely related to humanity" (Sahlins 1976:175). If this is true, and it seems exactly right, the same must also explain why cannibalism presents a problem to liberal American (and in general Western) anthropologists. There are ironies here. New Guinea peoples could well understand the kind of symbolic thinking Sahlins exposes, especially the point about dogs. The Hagen people, for example, say that dogs do have a mind, *noman*, because they do sometimes listen to what their "mother or father" (i.e., owners) say by guarding property for them. Yet, they point out, this *noman* is uncertainly established: dogs will steal, even from their owners. So indeed will pigs. The fact that dogs sometimes steal while pigs ordinarily do is in alignment with their relative edibility. Dog and pig are also synonymous in pejorative usage with incest, and witches, who are seen as cannibalistic, habitually appear as dogs. So for Hageners the symbolic world is in these regards rather similar to that of the average American, except that "dog" is divided into (1) a good aspect, the dog with *noman*, and (2) the bad dog as thief and witch, or cannibal, becoming "mindless" and so "turning back" to destroy society. As it happens, Hageners deplore cannibalism as much as Westerners do, but this is an accidental conjuncture, and we have no right to suppose that this must be a universal requirement for being properly human cross-culturally. It is, apparently, concern with problems created by the bias implied in the proposition "edibility is inversely related to humanity" that has led another American anthropologist, William Arens, to mount a fierce attack on the idea that some people are cannibals, dismissing it as a racist fantasy or colonialist propaganda and indicting anthropologists severely for perpetuating this "man-eating myth." Arens scores some very telling hits, to my mind, though I doubt his main conclusion that we have no real evidence that cannibalism was ever practiced, particularly with regard to New Guinea (see Wagner 1972; Koch 1974; Barth 1975). The point here, however, is that his whole concern starts from within the terms of Sahlins's proposition. He shows himself thus a true bearer of American culture. He is absolutely right to argue that popular images of the "savage" as cannibal are thinly disguised forms of insulting racism; and this was evidenced not long ago when a British team of explorers in New Guinea announced they had discovered a new "tribe" (fifteen people!) of supposed cannibals who had "never seen white men." The stuff of colonial myth was painfully revealed. As far as I can tell, the people were Hewa-speakers, and their culture was studied extensively by Lyle Steadman in the early 1970s. Steadman points out that the Hewa say they fear cannibal witches, mostly female, and that witchcraft is associated with a greed for meat. The ideas of witchcraft and cannibalism are thus used to control behavior. If so, the explorers were simply wrong. Their eagerness to attach labels without justification does, then, tell us about their worldview rather than about the people they found.

A final example of symbolic anthropology moves from witchcraft to terrorism, an easy shift. This topic, much in people's thoughts nowadays, when the politics of conflict are praised and those of consensus regarded as ideologically suspect and outmoded liberalism, has been handled both by the Berndts and Leach again. The Berndts's point is simple: the distinction between barbarian and civilized is a transposable symbol; therefore, it applies not analytically to any absolute set of cases but mutably and rhetorically, so those who oppose the rules of society from within, and by varying degrees of violence, become marked as "savages" by those who wish to uphold those rules. Inevitably, they are billed as nonpersons, or antipersons, as inhuman; hence, in turn they may be killed. Leach sets this out in a more structuralist way. First, he notes that legitimacy is a relative matter: "Whether we treat some other individual as a policeman or a criminal will depend on what we . . . *believe*. . . . A policeman endowed with the proper authority can legitimately break into a private house; a criminal can never do so. But legitimacy is always a matter of judgment rather than fact as the American Watergate Case showed all too clearly" (Leach 1977:16).

In practical terms, the question is how far can the ruler go before he destroys his legitimacy? Big-men often break rules, but if they follow the rules for breaking rules this may not be disastrous;

rather, it may enhance their prestige. But what if they also break the rules for breaking rules? From a different perspective, Leach goes on to argue that rulers are counterposed to criminals, as both are outside of the normal ambit of society. Either in practice may also be highly creative, and "human society would have died out long ago if it were not for the fact that there have always been inspired individuals who were prepared to break the rules." Such persons are anomalous, but the ruler draws legitimacy from God or society; yet if power flows the wrong way, and instead of the ruler dominating "we have the criminal terrorist dominating society by virtue of an illegitimate authority delegated by a factional group of revolutionaries," then legitimacies are clearly in conflict (Leach 1977:18). The merit of Leach's presentation is that it indicates that there is a structural aspect to terrorism. It is neatly expressed also in the African folktale about the rogue elephant whom Tortoise tamed by pretending to offer him the kingship, on account of his great power. The folktale ends comfortingly with the foolish beast collapsing into a hidden pit. Contemporary terrorists are unlikely to be lured so easily, but real reversals of incumbency underscore Leach's other point about legitimacy being a matter of judgment. Leach's moral is a liberal plea, also, in the face of events: "Our judges, our policemen and our politicians must never be allowed to forget that terrorism is an activity of fellow human-beings and *not* dog-headed cannibals" (1977:36).

These examples end on a rather serious note. There are other works that provide further witty or weighty excursions. Kenelm Burridge, for example, has written a case study of the relationship between anthropology and Australian aboriginal society that could be set alongside that of the Berndts. Feminist anthropologists have revealed the symbolic structures that underpin the role of "housewife" in British society (Oakley 1976). The sociobiological controversy, into which Sahlins has waded, throws us again into a consideration of universal and variant features of kinship which could follow my remarks about Schneider's view of American kinship (Sahlins 1977; Ruse 1979; Chagnon and Irons 1979). And Freddie Bailey has turned his satirical pen against academics themselves, giving the show away by pointing out their "stratagems and spoils" and their "morality," which turns out to be invariably tied to "expediency," and their "masks," too, which I have often thought should be kept hanging on pegs in rooms used for departmental meetings so that the faculty could reach for them, put them on and say "Speaking for the moment as Patron/Saint/Stroke/Buck/Reason/Sermon" or whichever mask was fitting to the argument. Bailey has also unerringly portrayed the role of departmental chairman as comparable to that of the head-man in colonial British Central Africa, occupying an uneasy inter-stitial position between his colleagues and his dean (1977:127–150, 184–191).

My main contention can, however, now be reiterated. Anthropology is not intrinsically about either the exotic or the familiar. Rather, it is about raising our consciousness, an aim that can be useful both in theoretical and applied topics. I would add one further point: fieldwork, as Roy Wagner argues, is the most likely means of achieving this aim, for it can force us both to understand other concepts and assumptions about the world, which have their own contextual validity and are not all reducible to ideology, and then bring to light buried assumptions in our own social life, which, being unrecognized, or even, as Pierre Bourdieu (1977) has so powerfully argued, in some cases "misrecognized," tend to dominate us without our knowing it. In this sense, whether one is a cultural relativist or not, the project of anthropology is ultimately liberal and universalist: to "know ourselves" and to "see ourselves as others see us." I end, then, with echoes from two heritages that have been important in forming my own "habitus" (Bourdieu's word): classical Greek thought and Scottish culture.

References

Arens, William
    1979   *The Man-Eating Myth.* Oxford University Press, New York.
Bailey, Frederick G.
    1977   *Morality and Expediency: The Folklore of Academic Politics.* Basil Blackwell, Oxford.
Barth, Fredrik
    1975   *Ritual and Knowledge among the Baktaman of New Guinea.* Yale University Press, New Haven.

Berndt, Catherine H., and Ronald M. Berndt
    1973 *The Barbarians: An Anthropological View.* Penguin Books, Har-
         mondsworth.
Bloch, Maurice
    1977 The Past and the Present in the Present. *Man* 12:278–292.
Bourdieu, Pierre
    1977 *Outline of a Theory of Practice.* Translated by R. Nice. Cambridge
         University Press, Cambridge.
Bourdillon, Michael F. C.
    1978 Knowing the World or Hiding It: A Response to Maurice Bloch.
         Man 13:591–599.
Burridge, Kenelm
    1973 *Encountering Aborigines: Anthropology and the Australian Aboriginal.*
         Pergamon Press, Oxford.
Chagnon, Napoleon A., and William G. Irons
    1979 *Evolutionary Biology and Human Social Behavior: An Anthropological
         Perspective.* Duxbury Press, North Scituate, Mass.
Cohen, Garry A.
    1978 *Karl Marx's Theory of History: A Defence.* Clarendon Press,
         Oxford.
Douglas, Mary, and Baron Isherwood
    1979 *The World of Goods: Towards an Anthropology of Consumption.* Allen
         Lane, London.
Dumont, Louis
    1977 *From Mandeville to Marx: The Genesis and Triumph of Economic Ide-
         ology.* University of Chicago Press, Chicago.
Gunder Frank, André
    1979 Anthropology = Ideology, Applied Anthropology = Politics. In
         *The Politics of Anthropology: From Colonialism and Sexism towards a
         View from Below,* edited by Gerrit Huizer and B. Mannheim, pp.
         201–214. Mouton, The Hague.
Habermas, Jürgen
    1979 *Communication and the Evolution of Society.* Translated by T. Mc-
         Carthy. Heinemann, London.
Hanson, F. Allan
    1979 Does God Have a Body? Truth, Reality and Cultural Relativism.
         Man 14:515–529.
Hsu, Francis L. K.
    1973 Prejudice and Its Intellectual Effect in American Anthropology:
         An Ethnographic Report. *American Anthropologist* 75:1–19.

Keiser, R. Lincoln
  1969 *The Vice Lords: Warriors of the Streets*. Holt, Rinehart and Winston, New York.
Leach, Edmund R.
  1961 *Rethinking Anthropology*. London School of Economics Monographs No. 22. Athlone Press, London.
  1977 *Custom, Law and Terrorist Violence*. Edinburgh University Press, Edinburgh.
Lienhardt, Godfrey
  1964 On the Concept of Objectivity in Social Anthropology. *Journal of the Royal Anthropological Institute* 94:1–10.
Llobera, Joseph R.
  1979 Techno-Economic Determinism and the Work of Marx on Pre-Capitalist Societies. *Man* 14:249–270.
Morauta, Louise
  1979 Indigenous Anthropology in Papua New Guinea. *Current Anthropology* 20:561–576.
Nakhleh, K.
  1979 On Being a Native Anthropologist. In *The Politics of Anthropology: From Colonialism and Sexism towards a View from Below*, edited by Gerrit Huizer and B. Mannheim, pp. 343–352. Mouton, The Hague.
Needham, Rodney
  1971 Introduction to *Rethinking Kinship and Marriage*. Association for Social Anthropology Monographs No. 11. Tavistock, London.
  1974 *Remarks and Inventions: Skeptical Essays about Kinship*. Tavistock, London.
Oakley, Ann
  1976 *Housewife*. Penguin Books, Harmondsworth.
Rey, Pierre P.
  1979 Class Contradiction in Lineage Societies. *Critique of Anthropology* 4(13 and 14):41–60.
Ruse, M.
  1979 *Sociobiology: Sense or Nonsense*. Episteme Vol. 8. D. Reidel, Dordrecht.
Sahlins, Marshall D.
  1976 *Culture and Practical Reason*. University of Chicago Press, Chicago.
  1977 *The Use and Abuse of Biology: An Anthropological Critique of Sociobiology*. Tavistock, London.

Salamone, Frank A.

    1979 Epistemological Implications of Fieldwork and Their Consequences. *American Anthropologist* 81:46–60.

Salmon, Merrilee H.

    1978 Do Azande and Nuer Use a Non-Standard Logic? *Man* 13:444–454.

Scheff, Thomas J.

    1977 The Distancing of Emotion in Ritual. *Current Anthropology* 18:483–506.

Schneider, David

    1968 *American Kinship: A Cultural Account.* Prentice-Hall, Englewood Cliffs, N.J.

Schutz, Alfred

    1970 *On Phenomenology and Social Relations.* Translated by H. Wagner. University of Chicago Press, Chicago.

Shweder, Richard

    1977 Likeness and Likelihood in Everyday Thought: Magical Thinking in Judgments and Personality. *Current Anthropology* 18:637–658.

Thompson, Edward P.

    1978 *The Poverty of Theory and Other Essays.* Merlin Press, London.

Wagner, Roy

    1972 *Habu: The Innovation of Meaning in Daribi Religion.* University of Chicago Press, Chicago.

    1975 *The Invention of Culture.* Prentice-Hall, Englewood Cliffs, N.J.

THREE

Fieldwork and Theory

in Social Anthropology

1981

I have chosen the topic of this chapter with two purposes in mind: first, to enable me to discuss some aspects of the history of social anthropology as a discipline, particularly arguments about whether it should be seen as a science on the model of the natural sciences or not; and second, because there has been for some time a debate about the place of fieldwork in anthropology, and this debate, in addition to its ethical and political dimensions, is closely related to the debate about the discipline's scientific status.

The reasons for this debate are historical, spanning the last twenty years, and as it happens this period coincides with the span of my own involvement with anthropology. Since 1964 I have spent a part of my time almost every year in field visits to two different language areas of the Central Highlands of Papua New Guinea. How does one situate a long-term project of this kind in terms of its contribution to a discipline? As it happens, the period of the project also marks a period in which social anthropology and history have moved much closer as disciplines after an epoch of divergence.

Reflections on the field thus take on the character of various kinds of history. It is important to realize that in a project of this sort the fieldwork itself is not a static thing; its character changes over time, both in accordance with prevailing interests in the

The material for this chapter is from my inaugural lecture as professor of Anthropology at University College London, given on March 18, 1981, although my appointment there began in 1976. A version of this lecture was published by the college later in 1981. Reprinted with permission of University College London.

subject as a whole, and in step with changes in the society being observed and the fieldworker's overall relationship with that society. From such continuing fieldwork it is possible to obtain a better historical sense: one that is related to this triple context of change, within one's subject or discipline, within the society studied, and within oneself (cf. Foster et al. 1979; Hymes 1969; Spindler 1970).

Fieldwork: Its Proponents and Attackers

British social anthropology took shape in the first half of the twentieth century under the powerful but disparate influence of two thinkers, Bronislaw Malinowski and Alfred R. Radcliffe-Brown. It was Malinowski for whom fieldwork was most important and who convinced his many students of its prime significance. His own extended period of fieldwork in the Trobriand islands of Papua took place during the First World War (Laracy 1976). His research on the family among Australian aborigines and on the Mailu of Papua had given him, prior to the Trobriands investigations, an idea of the theories he would apply to his data. He knew, too, that as an ethnographer he would be the "creator" of Trobriand society as an artifact of analysis (see also Sahlins 1976:76, 82). What is not clear is how he might have reconciled this aim with the potentially contradictory one he enunciated of understanding other cultures and representing them as from within, from the people's own viewpoint. This, via the more objective techniques of what he called "statistical documentation by concrete evidence" and observation of the "imponderabilia of actual life," was to be the "final goal, of which an Ethnographer should never lose sight." Malinowski writes: "To study the institutions, customs, and codes or to study the behavior and mentality without the subjective desire of feeling by what these people live . . . is, in my opinion, to miss the greatest reward which we can hope to obtain from the study of man." And also: "Perhaps through realizing human nature in a shape very distant and foreign to us, we shall have some light shed on our own" (1922:24).

Malinowski thus moves from a positivistic methodology to a humanistic aim by means of the paradoxes of the anthropological method of participant observation, which he did much to pioneer and publicize. His functionalism, which he similarly promoted, is related to these concerns. First, as is well known, he wanted to demolish the edifices of speculation on which an earlier version of anthropology had been built, in particular those evolutionist hypotheses for which contemporary tribal history was of interest only in so far as it exhibited characteristics which revealed the past history of society as a whole. The project here is two-fold: the rehabilitation of the object of analysis and the proper profession-alization of the subject discipline. In place of the "savage" created by the ideological writings of missionaries, he wished to build a picture of "well-ordered communities" whose coherence would demonstrate their viability and therefore warn the agents of colo-nial control not to tamper with them indiscriminately (1922:10). Malinowski was no revolutionary in his attitude toward colonized peoples, yet the implications of his point here were fundamental. His opposition to the doctrine of diffusionism, in which the ori-gins of customs were sought in first inventions which were sub-sequently diffused over wide areas, was of a piece with the rest of his thinking: such inventions and their spread might well be an aspect of social change, but one had still to study the degrees of integration of customs into specific social complexes at a given time. Such an insistence on local integrity can also be seen as enhancing the social stature of those studied, granting to them the genius of making themselves—socially and culturally if not technologically.

Throughout his writings, Malinowski was concerned with combating the erroneous views of his colleagues within the disci-pline of anthropology—or ethnology, as he called it—and it is ev-ident that his theoretical aims and polemics emerge from this context of historical combat within his own academic milieu, and not in any sense directly out of his Trobriand experience. Yet it is also artificial to separate these two spheres in any absolute sense. His choice of which views to take arms against undoubtedly was influenced by the data he had collected; and at the same time his data revealed the preoccupations and interests he took with him and developed during his fieldwork. It is a pity that Malinowski's posthumously published private diary (1967), which he had kept in Polish rather than English, reveals more about his emotional traumas and residual prejudices than about the progress of his ethnographic ideas in the field. This is simply because he clearly used the diary as an opiate and not as a record of his progress. We have to rely, rather, on the elaborately reconstructed statements found in the prefaces and first chapters of his numerous books. Whatever he himself suffered in the course of his fieldwork, he certainly impressed its necessity and value on his research students at the London School of Economics, and these went on to contribute notably to the creation of a corpus of ethnography of African, Melanesian, and Polynesian societies, for example Firth's famous work on Tikopia. Malinowski turned his own attention to "culture change" in African societies under British colonialism and, finally, to a last piece of fieldwork on markets in Mexico before he died of a heart attack in 1942. It has always seemed strange to me that he did not return to the Trobrianders for further fieldwork and for comparisons with his more superficial studies of African social change. Perhaps he had indeed "created" them and did not want the image to change, though I doubt that. In any event, many fieldworkers have, since the 1960s, been to the Trobriands area, and a host of field findings, based on Malinowski's own—extending or correcting them—has flowed into publication (e.g., Leach and Leach 1983; Weiner 1976).

The essential "fieldwork tradition," then, can be traced to Malinowski, as far as British social anthropology is concerned, just as it can to Franz Boas in the United States. Radcliffe-Brown was a thinker of a rather different stamp, who nevertheless is historically coupled with Malinowski by latter-day assessors. Let us note, initially, that the relationship between the two was polite but rather caustic. Radcliffe-Brown, in particular, from his chair at Oxford, tended to cite Malinowski only to disagree with him, and he especially poured scorn on Malinowski's later theory of biological needs as the basis of human society (Kuper 1977; Leach 1976; Fortes 1969).

Radcliffe-Brown wished to establish social anthropology even more strongly as a tight, self-sufficient discipline characterized by its own entirely scientific methods and findings. His aim was to formulate generalizations that ultimately would stand up as laws of society. The mode in which he worked was synchronic, typological, and comparative. Like Malinowski, Radcliffe-Brown was suspicious of conjectural history, holding that for the tribal societies studied by anthropologists nothing reliable about their history could be determined. Rather unlike Malinowski, he does not seem to have been interested in empathy with the people studied or in establishing an emic understanding of their lives. He had no experience comparable to Malinowski's. His major investigations in the Andaman Islands and among Australian aborigines were completed prior to Malinowski's, or at about the same time. And although he does discuss some of the effects of colonization on the Andamanese, his work lacks the characteristic Malinowskian footnotes of protest against the effects of social change despite the fact that disease, depopulation, and destructive relocation were much more marked in these field areas than they were in the Trobriands.

Radcliffe-Brown's outstanding contributions to his subject, in ethnographic terms, were emergent from his two main field projects but not intimately related to them, as were Malinowski's. This is because of the different theoretical projects they had in mind. Malinowski wanted to leave an enduring portrait of the Trobrianders; his portrait was so vivid it has gained for the Trobriands people a fame they, not having had the chance to oversee the painting, are not always impressed by. But it remains. To Radcliffe-Brown, the Andamanese were not a people to be immortalized in themselves; rather, they were to exemplify a theory, namely the theory that the function of ritual is to promote social solidarity. All details of meaningful action were ultimately related by him to this function, which thereby assumed the appearance of a "social law," even when in fact his interpretations are essentially post hoc and selective in character. In the case of the Australian aborigines, he took a different tack. Perhaps because it was evident to him that aboriginal societies were already less-than-functioning entities in themselves, he studied them comparatively and built a series of models of their systems of prescriptive marriage in terms of which their basic social structures could be understood and compared. Although he oversimplified the character of the local group, his overall typology was an enduring achievement and shows Radcliffe-Brown's brand of scientific method at its best. It is a piece of successful abstraction from field data that has fed into the general stream of our understanding, much as has Malinowski's Trobriand "portrait." (The level of abstraction exemplified is one which has subsequently been contested, in particular by Lévi-Strauss, who claims, of course, an approach by analogy with linguistic "deep structures" and their logic.) It is only when Radcliffe-Brown attempts to lift such well-founded regional generalizations to the level of general social laws that he either fails or becomes too simplistic. In other words, it is when he attempts to move, by inductive method, to the wider level, that the project cannot be sustained, any more than Malinowski's occasional guesses about "human nature" derived from his Trobriand data plus his own introspection can function as general theory.

It is interesting to note here that Radcliffe-Brown's concern with scientific method and theory is paralleled completely by that of his mentor, W. H. R. Rivers, yet the two came to hold radically different ideas about what theory should be applied to anthropological data. Rivers began, through his training in medicine at St. Bartholomew's hospital in London and his subsequent work in the psychology of perception and sensation, with a rigorous commitment to science as experimental method, and he retained a lifelong interest in the physiology of the nervous system, particularly in color vision and the perception of space. Through his work on Alfred Haddon's Torres Straits expedition, he was able to add the insight that perception is also culturally conditioned, and he anticipated by some sixty years the work of Brent Berlin and Paul Kay on the evolution of color nomenclature, doing so on the basis of his study of four Torres Straits languages, which Berlin and Kay have extended to 100 languages from different parts of the world (Berlin and Kay 1969). In ethnology itself, he insisted that his method of study of both kinship and oral history through the taking of careful genealogies from informants was what would put anthropology on a scientific footing (Slobodin 1978). The aim was to study not just custom but the structuring of custom. Rivers wrote in his influential posthumously published work that "social organization, fundamental as it is, and just because of this fundamental character, is unobtrusive. Its details only become apparent as the result of definite inquiry, while exact knowledge is hardly possible without the use of special methods." (1924:10–11)

In this, surely, Radcliffe-Brown and his teacher would be at one. Where they diverged sharply was in relation to the question of culture history. Rivers believed that previous phases of such history could be deduced from contemporary evidence, and that such history would also be scientific and would make an advance on the simpler hypotheses of the nineteenth-century cultural evolutionists. It seems that he was trying to find a middle ground between the historical particularism of Boas and the overarching speculations of Tylor and Frazer. Rivers's estimate of the reliability of results to be obtained by cultural-historical method was overoptimistic, but his conception of the kind of history that could be reconstructed was sound:

This form of history must always be on broad lines and will fail to deal with the personal relations which give to the study of history so much of its interest and charm. It may be noted, however, that the general tendency of recent movements in history has been in this direction. Every year more and more attention is being paid to history of institutions and ideas, while the personal relations and details of the transactions between individuals and nations are coming to be of less interest in themselves. (1922:28)

It is ironic that whereas Rivers's methods and substantive conclusions on Melanesian history have been much contested, his vision of the possible union between anthropology and history and between anthropology and psychology has survived his earlier eclipse by Radcliffe-Brown. Ironic also that Radcliffe-Brown's own principle applies here: there is a tendency in anthropology, just as much as in tribal societies, for there to be an alliance between alternate generations.

Whatever their differences, however, all of these anthropological pioneers believed firmly that fieldwork was important as a means of advancing properly grounded theory. But this position, too, was to be challenged. That challenge came from three sources:

the work of Ian C. Jarvie, carried out from the London School of Economics, where Malinowski taught before the war; the writings of Claude Lévi-Strauss in France; and critiques of colonialism, which implicated anthropologists and their kinds of fieldwork along with the colonial powers themselves—a critique which followed the transition of African colonies, in particular, to independence during the mid-1950s.

Jarvie is a philosopher and was a student of Ernest Gellner at the London School of Economics. He did not like the idea of fieldwork and developed his opposition to it extensively in terms of a claim that Malinowski had wrongly "killed" his predecessors in the subject, the broad thinkers of the nineteenth century, and that therefore the "fieldwork revolution" was false and was in fact inhibiting a proper return to the broad questions of the "psychic unity of the human species" or the overall evolution of society. He also criticized the logical faults of the systematized kind of structural-functionalism which came to be associated especially with Radcliffe-Brown, for example, the false explanation of antecedents by consequences. Instead, he argued, we should reinstate the human actor as choice-maker and study "situational logics": what makes sense to people at a given time and impels them to choose a course of action, and what are the unintended (or intended) consequences of these actions in history. He applied all this to a re-study of Melanesian cargo cults, using his ideas to criticize the analyses of those who had directly done fieldwork on such cults, such as Peter Lawrence, as well as those of rival theorists who had not done fieldwork on them, for example, Peter Worsely (Jarvie 1964).

Jarvie's attack and his solutions are neat, but in no way conclusive. His notion of situational logic depends on a prior construction of the society and culture which could only be obtained through orthodox field methods and analysis. His concept of unintended consequences leaves open to further investigation the question of whether institutions are supported or changed. Effectively, he was commenting on the end of the direct period of Malinowskian charisma and Radcliffe-Brownian domination. Thereafter new giants were sought out as father figures, and the two who were chiefly found were Lévi-Strauss and Marx.

Lévi-Strauss's fieldwork was in a minor key. It is quite definitely his independently operating intellect, rather than his field note-books, that give him his greatness. In one sense, his work followed that of Radcliffe-Brown, since his book on elementary systems of kinship is reminiscent of, and indeed draws on, the typology of marriage systems Radcliffe-Brown had made earlier. But Lévi-Strauss's scope is more vast, and his ambition is to provide an ev-olutionary scheme as well as to analyse the marriage systems of a region (Lévi-Strauss 1969). Overall, basing his ideas on an analogy with structural linguistics and with communications theory, he has attempted to set up anthropological theory at a systematic level of "deep structure." Since such deep structures are based on logical properties and for various reasons are always buried be-neath the surface of social life, direct observation is insufficient, if not quite powerless, to construct them. The empiricist approach to analysis has therefore to be discarded, but the comparative method is conserved. Other people's fieldwork becomes the raw data on which Lévi-Strauss works, as in his huge study of Amer-indian myths and their cross-cultural transformations and corre-spondences. This phase of Lévi-Strauss's work takes us further away both from fieldwork and from the study of history than his earlier work on marriage systems. Brilliant as it is, it is also some-times baffling and hard to replicate, even though the project ap-pears to verge on a "science of mythology." The most promising applications of his insistence on a logical approach appear to be in the properly mathematical realm of graph theory (Hage and Harary 1983). But in general the prestige of Lévi-Strauss's intellect has further dented the Malinowskian tradition.

To many, however, it is the third category of criticism that car-ries the most weight, for it points to the historical limitations of all work done in the social sciences, not just within social anthropol-ogy. The precise relationship between anthropological ideas, as expressed through fieldwork, and colonialism is itself deeply contested, and significantly so, especially since many of the facts are not well established (Asad 1973). But that there was some relationship should not be contested, for it is a matter of common sense to acknowledge this. The crudest version of the attack on the fieldworkers of the 1940s and 1950s and their mentors can be, for the most part, discounted: that is, that such anthropologists were simply agents of colonialism and capitalist interests embodied within it. On the contrary, they often vigorously opposed colonial laws, they regularly broke the taboos of colonial society and were therefore objects of suspicion; they initiated a practice of including the study of colonial officials and race relations into their fieldwork well before the critique of their role was invented; and their work, even when done on government funds, was as likely to be disregarded entirely by governments as used either for or against the peoples they studied. Both Rivers and Malinowski protested strongly against the abuse of Melanesian societies by the colonial powers. But it is not to this difficult and complex ethical aspect of history that I wish to draw attention. It is rather to the fact that anthropologists were inevitably influenced, perhaps unconsciously, by the worldview of their times, and this perhaps led to two features in their writings: an emphasis on the synchronic stability of institutions rather than their historical transformations and a lack of development of tools by means of which to examine the wider encompassing structures of history within which colonized societies were encapsulated. It is these two deficiencies that the newer, post-colonial approaches have attempted to remedy, if for no other reason than that the life of tribespeople is obviously bound up with the existence of nation-states and international relations between these states. In truth, this has been the case ever since such states existed and Western expansion into other parts of the world began. I merely stress that now the involvement is more apparent. Aspects of it were clear enough to me when, as a graduate student, I began to do fieldwork in New Guinea in 1964, the year in which Jarvie's book "against fieldwork" was published.

Fieldwork and Theory: Four Cases

Before directly taking up discussion of the New Guinea project, however, I want to consider some other cases of ethnographic studies and investigate the relationship exhibited in them between the authors' fieldwork and the theories they deploy to explain their findings.

To anticipate the conclusion here, some of the most accomplished and interesting of field monographs nevertheless show awkward forms of disjunction between their data and their theories; yet it is precisely in this area of disjunction that creative criticism and reformulation can take place. Rarely is there a case so simple as to correspond to the "hypothesis-falsification" model of positivistic science. Nor yet, on the other hand, do anthropologists in the field find "real societies" corresponding to ideal types. What, then, are we trying to do? One approach here is to affect a straightforward modesty and to content ourselves with saying that anthropology has little to do with "grand theory," as Adam Kuper argues. He represents grand theory as various theories of social "reality," that ultimate reality which should form a focus of theorizing (Kuper 1980). The roots of this matter he locates in the Malinowskian revolution as it applied to fieldwork and the difficulty of making comparisons on the basis of ethnographies written precisely in order to capture the unique, interconnected details of a given case. Exit from the problem is made via the idea of structure, represented as paradigm or model, but the middle-level concepts so created still do not reach to the more overarching concepts of theory as such. If this is true, it might appear as though theory has to spring fully armed, like Athena from the head of Zeus, and thence move forward to confront the lowly masses of data which advance out of field notebooks, asserting her divine right to rule over them by a twirl of her sword: theory as the bold heroine taming fact.

This is too extreme a formulation. Yet it points out sharply the fact that there is a problem, and a recurring one at that.

My first example of this problem is the work of Radcliffe-Brown on the Andaman Islanders, first published in 1922 but based on fieldwork carried out in 1906–1908 when its author held an Anthony Wilkin Studentship at Cambridge. (This was founded in the name of Anthony Wilkin, who died while on fieldwork in Egypt after taking part in the Cambridge anthropological expedition to the Torres Straits in 1898.) The long gap between fieldwork and publication probably reflects an alteration in perspective on Radcliffe-Brown's part. Indeed, Radcliffe-Brown tells us as much in his preface to the 1932 edition, where he writes:

In 1908–9, when the writing of this book was undertaken, anthropologists and ethnologists were concerned either with formulating hypotheses as to the origins of institutions or with attempts to provide hypothetical reconstructions of the details of culture history. . . . It was largely from this point of view that I approached the study of the Andaman Islanders. . . . The appendix on technology in this book is an example of what was intended. (1932:vii)

What is this appendix? It is a rather careful account of the material culture of the Andamanese done with a view to reconstructing a proto-Andaman culture that could then be compared with the Semang of the Malay Peninsula and the Aeta of the Philippines, on the grounds that these all represented fragments of a single people, the Negritos, putatively related to those who also colonized New Guinea and Australia some 40,000 years ago. This ethnological approach was derived from that of Rivers, whose large work on the history of Melanesian society had been published in 1914. Rivers puts forward in this a number of hypotheses about Melanesian origins, such as that of "kava people" and "betel people" and his idea that kin terminology could be used to reconstruct past practices of marriage. Although he launched his interpretations from carefully recorded data, they certainly succumb to the stricture of "conjectural history." Radcliffe-Brown does not tell us in any detail how he came to the conclusion that this ethnological approach was unprofitable. At any rate, his own writing was delayed. He does say directly that the solution for him came from the work of French sociologists centered on Emile Durkheim; and in particular one may extrapolate that it was Durkheim's *The Elementary Forms of Religious Life* (1912) that swayed him (1932:325). Radcliffe-Brown never specifically reproduced Durkheim's main thesis that religion is the worship of society itself appearing in a divine form. Avoiding such a grand claim, he nevertheless took his basic interpretative standpoint from Durkheim and proceeded to account for his ethnographic "facts" in terms of the idea that rituals function to promote group solidarity and to remind individuals of their necessary dependence on the group.

Two details fall into place here. The first is that in his book Radcliffe-Brown rigorously separates his "description" from "interpretation." The description is presented naturalistically, although it obviously includes a good deal of analysis and generalization about Andamanese society which is in fact crucial in its contribution to the later interpretations. Second, he writes, "It may be worth while to mention that the interpretation of Andamanese customs . . . was not worked out until after I had left the islands. Had it been otherwise I should have made careful enquiries into subjects which, as it was, escaped my notice" (1932:231).

Elsewhere Radcliffe-Brown tantalizingly notes that he tried to use the genealogical method, propounded by Rivers, but failed with it owing to his inexperience (72), and he confesses, too, that at the time he was in the field he failed to realize the importance of a thorough understanding of the people's ideas on sex, and so did not make enough enquiries about these ideas (322)—unlike Malinowski and unlike Rivers, too, who discusses sexual practices and ideas at length for the Todas of the Nilgiri hills in a book published in 1906.

These are only fragments, but they seem to be honest fragments, and they reveal the fact that the data were originally gathered with an entirely different object in view from the use to which they were in fact put in the interpretive section of Radcliffe-Brown's book. Small wonder that the work was a considerable time in gestation. We are not told, though, whether the bulk of the interpretation was written before 1914 or only shortly before eventual publication in 1922.

Several further comments are also in order. The ethnographer was able to use his data in this way, even though it also demonstrated to him some notable gaps and limitations in his knowledge. As later readers, we can also use his remarks about failures in fieldwork to feed into a reinterpretation of what he wrote. The remark about genealogies is noteworthy here, given the lack of unilineal descent rules among the people studied. Probably genealogies did not function as charters to delimit groups, although they may have been important for other purposes, such as the transmission of personal names. Radcliffe-Brown did not use his new-found Durkheimian insight, however, to make a return visit to the Andamanese and further test out his ideas or complete his data. Still, contrary to Adam Kuper's argument, the ethnographer in this case definitely did benefit from "grand theory," that is from Durkheim. Indeed, this theory removed him from an impasse in his thinking and set the foundations for all of his later work. It is possible that Radcliffe-Brown's shift away from the ethnological approach was all the sharper for the fact that it did not come from his fieldwork itself but from reflection on that fieldwork. It was not influenced by any practical field difficulties, but with the equally practical problem of giving shape and meaning to the account of his findings. In my view this experience is rather common in social anthropology.

I am not here concerned to criticize Radcliffe-Brown's interpretations of Andamanese ritual. Such criticisms have been made often enough, although more with respect to their general functionalist orientation than to their plausibility of detail with respect to Andamanese society and culture. The data are, in fact, detailed enough to permit one to build a further analysis in addition to the pointers provided by the author. As might be expected in the area of myth and ritual, a structuralist approach, following the orientation of Lévi-Strauss, can be used to understand the significance of the goddess Biliku, the seasons, the relationship of earth to sea, and the colors red, white, and grey used for self-decoration. But again, that is not my purpose. Rather, I am concerned to show the paradoxical combination of disjunction and unity between fieldwork and theory in the case of Radcliffe-Brown, moving next to the case of Edward Evans-Pritchard and his study of the Nuer, based on fieldwork carried out in three visits between 1930 and 1936.

The Nuer case is also instructive. The ethnography has been subjected to much more intensive scrutiny than happened to Radcliffe-Brown, partly because Evans-Pritchard continued to work on and teach about his Nuer materials for many years, producing a trilogy of books, the last published in 1956. It was the first of these, *The Nuer*, which was most widely influential in that it developed a picture of Nuer politics as based on an interplay between a territorial system, which Evans-Pritchard regarded as basic, and a segmentary lineage system, equally basic. Neither was seen simply as a "reflection" of the other, but in political terms the lineage system and the territorial system were pictured as intertwined through the dogma of the dominant clan in each tribal territory, and alliances and opposition were expressed in the famous pattern of fission and fusion formed by the calculation of social distance via the genealogical nodes of the descent system. As a type-case for the segmentary lineage concept this picture of the Nuer, fascinating as it was, was also rather unfortunate. The particular interplay between territory and descent in the Nuer case is somewhat unusual, and it cannot be properly explained without an examination of certain historical circumstances, notably the Nuer's expansion against their neighbors, the Dinka, and their own suffering at the hands of Arab slave-traders and traders living to their north during the nineteenth century (Holy 1979; Kelly 1985; Sacks 1979). It was left to Meyer Fortes, rather than Evans-Pritchard, to elaborate in general analytical terms a model of unilineal descent group structures that would be of sufficient generality to apply to a wide set of cases in Africa. And this model, in turn, produced difficulties when extended to Melanesia. More recently, it has seemed profitable to apply Melanesian models of big-manship back to the analysis of Nuer local communities, since we find that leadership in these is based as much on personal assertiveness and the ability to attract followers, rewarding them with cattle, as on criteria arising from personal birth status.

Like Radcliffe-Brown, Evans-Pritchard leaves few clues as to how he arrived at his analysis of Nuer society. Given the style of fieldwork in the 1930s, it is unlikely that he had any sharp hypotheses at the outset; and his work was hampered greatly by a harsh physical environment, his own sicknesses, and the fact that the Nuer had recently been bombed by the Anglo-Egyptian government and were hostile to outsiders. Yet he won them over; and they in turn finally stopped him from doing systematic fieldwork by engaging in incessant social visiting and friendly badinage (something I experienced also in New Guinea). It appears safe, therefore, to argue that in his case, too, the analysis is almost entirely an artifact of his later reflections on the data, aided by discussions with his Oxford colleagues, who then included both

Radcliffe-Brown and Meyer Fortes. This circumstance produces the same two effects as noted for the Andamans study: gaps appear in the analysis when further questions are asked, yet the data are also sufficient at least to raise the possibility of numerous further interpretations. Both the shortcomings of the study and its strengths can be seen; the combination of these is characteristic. Evans-Pritchard was also acutely aware of the limitations of his analysis, not so much at the level of data but in terms of its theoretical mode of exposition. He argued that we must move beyond discussion in terms of tribes, clans, villages, and the like and use these concepts of social groupings "to denote relations, defined in terms of social situations, and relations between these relations" (1940:266). There is an unmistakably mathematical ring about this idea, but he never followed it up. He writes also, movingly, of "vast stretches" of intellectual country before him, and he sees how he would like to traverse them but cannot.

From the 1960s onwards those stretches were covered by rival bands of explorers, an army of -isms, invading anthropology from all sides. I doubt if this is what Evans-Pritchard himself envisaged, though surely his pursuit of the abstract found its answer at least partly in Lévi-Strauss's work.

In the rejection of functionalism there was, in British social anthropology of the 1960s, a turning towards the study of meanings, in which a quickened interest in Lévi-Strauss finds its place. It is ironic to reflect that meaning was itself a major preoccupation of Radcliffe-Brown's early Andamans study; just as, in quite a different way, it was fundamental to Malinowski's ideal of grasping the Trobrianders' view of their world. So meaning was always there, underlying the question of observed or imputed functions. It has come to the fore in two quite different ways, which show how the old dilemmas are still present in the struggle for theory in social anthropology. A revivified Marxism applied to pre-capitalist societies has had to come to grips with the particular forms of belief, custom, and ritual in these societies in the effort to understand how such factors stand vis-à-vis the Marxist concepts of relations of production, forces of production, superstructure, and infrastructure. Conversely, the phenomenology of Husserl, broadened by the work of Alfred Schutz, has been invoked by some writers as the means of realizing Malinowski's ideal, and at the same time avoiding or refusing the step towards universalist concepts which Marxists and, differently, structuralists insist on taking. A brief characterization of two ethnographies will support my assertions here.

The first is David Labby's book *The Demystification of Yap: Dialectics of Culture on a Micronesian Island* (1976). Yap belongs to the Western Carolines in the American-administered Trust Territory of the Pacific Islands. In common with other Micronesian peoples, inhabitants of this region practice matrilineal descent: clan membership is obtained solely through the mother; and, in common with most Polynesian societies, there is an emphasis on differential rank between "high" and "low" people. Rank does not adhere to the matrilineal clans as such, but rather to a series of landed estates; inheritance of these is obtained through one's father, not one's mother. Upon marriage, a woman moves to her husband's place and bears children for him there. The children socially reproduce their mother's clan, but they stay at the father's place; the sons will speak, as the Yapese say, with the voice that their father's land and its ancestral spirits gives them. By marrying a man of rank and moving onto his estate, a woman can improve the effective standing of her clan. Women are thus described graphically as "navigators" who steer their canoes to a new place; men are like "mooring stones," fixed in one position.

What are the Marxist—or, more generally historical materialist—elements which Labby brings to play in this analysis? First, he speaks of a dialectic between the ideology of the clan and that of the estate. As often happens, the idea of a "dialectic" is more rhetorically attractive than it is clear. The context in which it is said to occur is that of marriage. There is no bridewealth payment, but when a woman marries a man she is said by the people to "hook" his estate inheritance for her own clan. She does so only by becoming pregnant and producing children for him while on that estate land, and she pays for this by her labor on her husband's taro gardens. She herself is said to be like a garden on which the husband works to implant children. At the same time, as we have seen, she is like a navigator and a fisherman in terms of her own search for land and status. In other words, the disjunction between matrilineal descent and patrifilial inheritance of land and rank is mediated by the exchanges that take place in marriage. And, as Labby points out, the cultural idea of the significance of labor is important: the ancestors provided land with a "voice" because they, too, invested labor in it and thus gave it standing. This account of the significance of land and the author's realization that land was the focus of what his informants were discussing are what give the work its materialist flavor, but its use of Marxist ideas is distinctly muted. Determinism does not enter the account; exploitation is not posited; only dialectics and historical process remain, and these are not exclusive to Marxism. The real clue to the whole approach comes at the beginning of the book, where Labby notes that he began by reacting against what he thought of as the static mentalism of Lévi-Strauss's work.

> I should . . . note that although the analysis uses the terms of historical materialism . . . I did not set out to "do" a Marxist analysis. . . . I began simply with a dissatisfaction with Lévi-Straussian structuralism. . . . But I had only the vaguest notion of how this could be overcome . . . (1976:11)

He goes on to say that his understanding of historical materialism has been to a considerable extent created through working on the Yapese materials, and at the same time the materials "seemed to demand" such an approach. This sort of interaction between ethnography and theory is precisely of the kind already noted. In passing, it is also worth saying of Labby's study that a good deal of Lévi-Strauss's approach is still embedded within it, for example, in his use of a doubtful nature/culture opposition. This tends to confound the materialist approach itself, for if land is material it nevertheless figures largely in the account also as a constructed idea. The upshot is that in this confrontation between materialist theory and the apparent "facts" of a precapitalist society, it is the latter that seems to require modification of the former. Influence, however, is not one way but reciprocal, and it is here that we find, perhaps, the dialectic that shapes the way, in practice, that the discipline of social anthropology achieves its progress. (For more reflections on Yap, see Schneider 1984.)

The second example comes from the Philippines. It is Michelle Rosaldo's study, *Knowledge and Passion: Ilongot Notions of Self and Social Life* (1980). In keeping with her phenomenological approach, this ethnographer's problem explicitly includes the author herself. It is this: given the fact that the author and her husband felt close to their Ilongot friends, how could they reconcile such a feeling of closeness with the fact that these people had been, until very recently, headhunters for whom it was a supreme, indeed necessary, expression of angry manhood to sever the head of an enemy? The problem required a vigorous and sustained pursuit of the meaning of headhunting for these people, such that the central act would be set into a nexus of values and thus understood. Sensitive to the difficulties of translation and concerned to convey meanings as expressed by the Ilongot themselves, Rosaldo sets all of the crucial terms of her description within inverted commas. English provides poor glosses for Ilongot semantics; everything has to be understood in a special sense. At the heart of the account, however, there stand two fundamental oppositions based on age and sex: senior men are characterized by knowledge, which gives them patience, the ability to mediate and manipulate; junior men are expected to show *liget*, passion, and to express this by taking a head before they marry. In so doing the junior men also define themselves as different from women. Male chauvinism is involved, as well as a juxtaposition of the generations:

> Neither good nor evil in itself, liget suggests the passionate energy that leads young men to labor hard, to marry, kill and reproduce; but also if ungoverned by the "knowledge" of mature adults, to engage in wild violence. . . . The young lack "knowledge" just as the old lack "force," and women, considered fearful and thus inclined to stay at home, cannot attain the heights of wisdom or of liget that are enjoyed by men (Rosaldo 1980:27)

One senses the familiar note of ideology here; but Rosaldo is not concerned to denounce it as mystification. Rather, she wishes to set these ideas more and more into their context: first, by a meticulous and sustained exposition of Ilongot concepts which construct the idea of the Ilongot person; second, by following the application of these concepts in daily life, including, for example, "the imagery of hunting and horticultural magic, and . . . the organization of productive labor." Rosaldo's aim is to show the interaction between ordinary conduct and concepts, and how "these concepts shape people's understandings and evaluations of everyday action and turn potentially problematic expressions of male dominance into the obvious and inevitable consequences of everyday life" (1980:100).

The enquiry thus runs deep, examining the assumptions of Ilongot culture not just through an abstract analysis of ideas, nor yet simply in case histories of action, but by showing minutely the way that concepts enter into action and the evaluation of action. Throughout, although the discussion largely centers on concepts of emotions, Rosaldo makes it plain that she is talking about cultural configurations, shared notions, about the means of communication as well as the means of self-expression in the society. The effect is, literally, one of insight, of a very particular vision realized by both ethnographer and people. It is not till the end that Rosaldo looks up from the Ilongot case and considers whether her study has any wider implications. She leaves the reader with an interesting suggestion:

> Although killing involves such shared assumptions as the promotion of male dominance in marriage and the relative subordination of unmarried youths, it is also in young headhunters that old men see, revitalized, their lives. If headhunting is a sort of initiation . . . its deeper resonances lead . . . much less toward magical and cosmological concerns than to the hopes of elders to assure the reproduction of their groups in the face of the inevitable facts of aging and decline. (1980:231)

Rosaldo moves thus from the particular to the general, noting at the end an important point: that even the account of the particular has to be informed by certain general concerns, so that "the translation of particulars is at once a way of probing a distinctive . . . form of life and an exercise in the comparative study of human societies" (233).

In its concern with meanings as socially produced and its focus on concepts of emotion as the source of society rather than on concepts of social control, Rosaldo's book is a highly successful and thought-provoking piece of ethnographic theorizing. She has "buried" her theory deeply in the ethnography itself, by insisting that a study of the "exotic" is best carried out through a relentless and aware pursuit of its everyday and "unexotic" realities.

It is in this regard, then, that Rosaldo's study is phenomenological. And as it links, therefore, directly with Schutz's work, it shows us again that while the anthropologist may well proceed inductively and by hesitant steps to put data together in the form of analysis, there are plenty of opportunities, in the end, to make connections with general social theory. My only criticism of Rosaldo's work is that she has, in a sense, succeeded too well in presenting her study as a set of indigenous "meanings," since she has ruled out the possibility of other kinds of explanations of the Ilongot practice of headhunting.

Fieldwork in Papua New Guinea

When I arrived in Mount Hagen in early 1964, I already knew that the Highlands societies, although only recently discovered by Europeans, had experienced rapid forms of social change: colonial pacification, the building of roads, evangelization by Catholic and Lutheran missionaries, the introduction of huge numbers of shell valuables to pay for goods and services, the export of laborers to work on the coast, the creation of local government councils, alienation of land for plantations, the beginnings of smallholder coffee growing, the imposition of trials for offenses against administrative and criminal regulations, direct government by visiting Australian patrol officers, the purchase of foodstuffs and clothing from European and Chinese stores—all of these matters were either already underway or were just beginning. I also knew that there had been many modifications in the local social structure, first outlined by Lutheran and Catholic missionaries in their writings on Mount Hagan (Vicedom and Tischner 1943–48; Strauss and Tischner 1962). One matter was of particular interest: the indigenous exchange system (*moka*) had not been abandoned but had effloresced since colonial control. I thus had a set of ethnographic and historical baselines from which to work. I was freed, even before beginning, from attempting to reconstruct a synchronic picture of the society and was forced to consider questions of historical continuity and alteration.

Certain frameworks which constrained and informed my work were therefore evident from the beginning and were built into the research design. But others were not. I tried to maintain a broad front in my studies, since this is one of the virtues of the anthropological approach, though also a potential trap. For some topics I undoubtedly had a better training than others. The problem I had set myself before entering the field had to do with a debate relating to Evans-Pritchard's study of the Nuer. Anthropologists working in colonial conditions in African societies had produced a notable series of models of segmentary lineage systems derived from the approaches of Evans-Pritchard and Fortes and had buttressed these by reference to the construct of the corporate group, earlier theorized by Sir Henry Maine and Max Weber. From all this they distilled a set of general propositions about unilineal descent groups, supposedly characteristic of a large set of societies. Radcliffe-Brown himself initiated this trend by stressing the significance of unilineal descent in his typologies of African systems—another paradox, perhaps, since the Andamanese, whom alone he had studied in detail, had no such descent groups. The newly studied New Guinea Highlands systems seemed to be throwing up features that did not correspond to those well-chiseled and carefully elaborated African models. What was one to make of it? Earlier studies suggested that in practice the key to the problem was to understand ranges of flexibility and how these were to be related to matters such as warfare, availability of land, and patterns of leadership. The ethnographic categories and the problem were thus fairly well defined in advance. What the field study itself taught me was that further insight can be obtained from understanding properly what the people's own categories are, as features of their language, and then examining how they use these as rhetorical counters in contexts of everyday life. From this I learned how difficult it is to grasp such categories and translate them adequately, and also that flexibility inheres precisely in their rhetorical use in practical contexts. In brief, semantics and pragmatics have both to be considered, and the study of a category such as "descent" requires us both to develop "concrete documentation" of numbers of cases, as Malinowski argued, and to appreciate that their significance is entirely dependent on the meaningful categories in terms in which people discuss them, as Rosaldo has since shown for the Ilongot concept of *liget* (A. J. Strathern 1971, 1972).

My other major area of study, which still continues as a preoccupation, was that of ceremonial exchange. One of the distinctive features of Highlands societies in Papua New Guinea is their tremendous development of forms of such exchange. Here, a comparative viewpoint is in order, for such exchanges are of the kind documented extensively by Malinowski and by Boas, on the Kwakiutl Indians of North America, and written about brilliantly, shortly after Malinowski's findings were published, by the French sociologist Marcel Mauss in his book *Essai sur le don*. What more, therefore, did we need to know? Highlands systems show, to a greater extent than the Trobriands or Kwakiutl cases, the development of a flourishing system of leadership that did not depend on any prior definition of aristocratic lineages as eligible to compete for status, still less on any rigid rule of succession to such leadership. At the same time, there were historical opportunities for pragmatic forms of strengthening one's hold on power and of consolidating it over more than one generation. The complex varieties of leadership which could thus emerge have led anthropologists into arguments about whether these systems were characterized by anarchy or, to the contrary, despotism, and also about how these systems have been affected by social change. In fact, they could be marked by both anarchy and despotism, but more often had neither. There were both pressures controlling potential despots (not least assassination) and stimuli favoring the reproduction of influence. Descent-group theory was inadequate to handle all this, and hypotheses about personal leadership had to be brought into play. The institutional framework was provided by the rules of an elaborate and competitive system of gift-giving in which influence resulted from giving away more wealth than others and progressively calling in one's credits, only to mount up greater debts. Volatility is the hallmark here; and good progress could be made by gradually analyzing the individual strategies that big-men adopted to raise the pigs and shell valuables they needed and to counter the challenges of their rivals. At the same time, these exchanges also expressed intergroup relations of enduring alliance, with a structural duration greater than that of individual life spans, although changes could be discerned in these alliance patterns since colonial pacification.

In his criticism of fieldwork as practiced in the 1950s, Jarvie went to Melanesian data in order to argue for the importance of studying individual action as a focus of social change. Naturally, he could not have done so if field studies had been unavailable. While I had no idea of his work when I went to the field, it appeared afterwards to me as though he and I had reached similar conclusions by entirely different routes. I had the same initial reaction when I read Fredrik Barth's brief study *Models of Social Organization* (1966). Barth also emphasized choice, and his arguments gave birth to the version of exchange theory subsequently known as transactionalism. The difficulty with both approaches is that in no way do they enable us to dispense with the study of the frameworks which constrain choice, whether in practical, material terms or in terms of the limitations imposed by political power or cultural worldview. In studying New Guinea exchange systems, I have indeed been concerned to trace exactly how inequality is generated out of equality by the exercise of individual choice, but it would be quite wrong to argue therefore that the whole social system is simply an artifact of such choices. What we have to come to terms with in the study of society is the emergent nature of the phenomena we are dealing with. Individual action feeds into a wider set of constraints and becomes meaningful only in relation to these. Action is therefore neither culturally dictated nor entirely an individual product, and any theory that plumps for an oversimplification either in the direction of cultural determinism or by appealing simply to the idea of individual freedom is bound to fail. (I would further argue that the reasons for this circumstance are rooted in the longer-term evolution of human society, and that therefore in the end there can be no hard and fast distinction between social anthropology and physical anthropology in terms of their ultimate objects of analysis.)

Highlands societies have experienced long-term transformations, and realization of this point has brought me into closer acquaintance with the work of archaeologists. This has become possible through the work of Professor Jack Golson, who has carried out his own field investigations in a part of the territory occupied by the small tribe with which I have been living and working. Golson's fine investigations show an astonishingly long and complex history of established agriculture in the Highlands, going back perhaps as far as 9,000 years ago and preceded by hunter-gatherer settlements from some 30,000 years ago. The dates of archaeological phases can be established by means of layers of volcanic ash which fell at intervals of time, the latest coinciding with the point at which the swampy area where the digging has been carried out was last abandoned in favor of the hilly grasslands nearby. Patterns of change in the intensity of use of the high-fertility drained peatlands in the swamp vary probably in accordance with the type of staple crop grown. The sweet potato tuber, perhaps introduced some 300 years before the present, enabled a growing dispersal of population up the hillsides to take place, since sweet potato yields better at higher altitudes than the previous taro and yam crops, which are still grown in reduced quantities. The sweet potato probably also enabled greater numbers of pigs to be kept, and it also contributed both to the development of population pressure on land, fighting, and the escalation of competitive exchanges between groups as a ritualized method of controlling warfare. High intensity and high productivity social systems such as that which thus developed in Mount Hagen can be found throughout the central Highlands valleys and uplands; and they are surrounded by systems in which there is lesser intensification, and these by peripheral systems in which there is greater reliance on sago collection, gathering in general, limited horticultural cultivation, and the hunting of wild pigs. In other words, it is possible to begin building a picture of regional micro-evolution using a combination of archaeological, ecological, and social anthropological studies and techniques. It is this "residential complex," to use the phrase of Harold Brookfield, a human geographer who has worked in the Highlands, which has then to be considered the immediate context in which the effects of colonial penetration have been felt (Golson 1982).

My gradually altering perspective on the area has made me acutely aware of the limitations of our knowledge. The archaeological record has barely begun to be established; in the contemporary world social change is so swift and widespread that several field projects would be needed to locate the data needed to understand patterns of regional change. On the basis, however, of my shorter visits since 1975, I have been able to produce some useful sketches of processes of transformation. In this context, a new debate has taken the place of earlier ones which centered on questions of descent and big-man styles of leadership. Now anthropologists are arguing about the effects of "under-development." Are Hageners and New Guinea Highlanders in general becoming peasants on their own land as a result of their involvement in cash-cropping? How is money absorbed into the local exchange system? The influx, first of shell valuables and then of money, has enabled a great efflorescence of exchange activities to take place, yet commitment to the ethic underpinning such exchanges is also being steadily eroded in favor of commodity production. Clearly this is a point at which the local circumstances of the Mount Hageners become meshed with those of their nation and the world at large; yet this does not mean that they can be adequately understood only by referring to the wider context. As with everything, an interactive viewpoint is required, one which replaces mechanical determinism with an awareness of variation (A. J. Strathern 1982).

Another issue runs beneath these tasks of documentation and analysis. This is the need to ensure that ethnography can become more reflective and can answer to some of the people's concerns as well as to the concerns of social anthropology. I have tried to meet this in various ways, particularly by publishing translations of texts and songs that friends in the field have wanted to see preserved. This is a very much underexplored area in anthropological writing, and one that is bound to become more crucial as time goes on.

My realization of the problems here derives partly from periods spent teaching in Papua New Guinea and partly from repeated returns to the field itself. As the anthropologist becomes better known in a field area—for example, as his own aging process becomes evident to the people studied—he then acquires for them, as they do reciprocally for him, a sharper social identity as an individual. The need both to place yourself socially and to express yourself individually becomes stronger. You move, therefore, more obviously in their world, as well as looking at it and asking about it. And the more you do so the more the assumption that the relationship is permanent is strengthened. This is a classic crux in participant observation. Once a society becomes familiar and the researcher is comfortable in it and ceases to study it as anything refractory or difficult, in a sense he or she just lives there instead. In that case one is no longer doing fieldwork. In the case of my own work the feeling of familiarity is fortunately jolted at regular intervals both by the pace of change and by the reality of working in two or more different languages, so the unfamiliar is continually reasserting itself and requiring study. What has, of course, become a part of me is the feeling of matching my own life and activities to the requirements of such a study, renewed both by change in the society and by change in the discipline, and these continuously mediated by the observer as the instrument of observation, understanding, and communication.

What I have said here bears insertion into the wider debates about whether anthropology is or is not a science, what its overall aims are, induction versus deduction, whether fieldwork is a means to discovery or simply a mirror reflecting the fieldworker's ideology, and so on. These are all debates which have grown up in the last twenty years, and they relate to genuinely difficult issues. However, the dichotomies suggested are usually inadequate to grasp the problems posed, because the complexities of fieldwork experience simply transcend them. The fieldworker is not different from the thinking person, student, or lecturer. Fieldwork is a part of that person's total involvement, and in that sense reflects all of the person's bundle of ideas, hypotheses, biases, interests, insights, scientific excellence, or whatever. We have to concentrate, I think, on the instrument, which is this bundle that is the person;

and on the task or project, which may converge more or less toward the pole of natural science in terms of its aims and methods, with an infinitely varying interplay between what is known "before" and "after" the fieldwork. This is especially so with repeated visits to the same field areas such as I have been involved in. In that case, to ask whether one is using an inductive or deductive method is beside the point if presented as a simple either/or proposition; but it is still possible and meaningful to ask what the methodological basis of a particular piece, or phase, of work is and how it relates to an author's overall orientation.

In social anthropology we are now confronted with an embarrassment of riches in terms of theory. Since the first decision to label a particular historical phase "structural-functionalism," those who affixed that label have gone on to affix many more labels to themselves and others. It is an exercise which operates in some ways as a teaching aid, in others as a dangerous oversimplification. One difficulty is actually created by the labeling process: anyone who does not adhere clearly to a given -ism is liable to be stigmatized with the residual label of "eclecticism." But what is concealed thereby is the fact that, for purposes of critical evaluation of theories, it is actually necessary to move across the divisions posited. Second, the label also refuses to recognize the fact that the subject of social anthropology throws up a variety of problems, and these actually require us to take up methods and perspectives from more than one tradition of writing and thought. What is necessary to bear in mind is that a casual combination of modes of reasoning from such different traditions can defeat the purpose of critical analysis by rendering one's account incoherent. Styles and assumptions must therefore be carefully distinguished; but, equally, it is wrong to equate the discipline as a whole with any one of them. In this connection, it is also interesting to observe that the proliferation of recent approaches to theory has not seemingly generated a corresponding proliferation of fieldwork methods.

For the future, I should like to make two observations on the potentialities of our subject. One is its application to complex, industrialized societies. Two widely different approaches present themselves here: to regard social anthropology as essentially encapsulating a method of study of small-scale phenomena, and therefore to choose correspondingly small social fields for intensive observation; or to develop or adopt theories which will enable us to conceptualize complex societies in themselves, in which case social anthropology merges with general social theory. I do not see why both strategies should not be pursued, especially since the workings of society-wide forms of ideology, for example, can often be best understood by seeing how they work in micro between small numbers of persons.

The second observation is on the potential "reversibility" of social anthropology. If it is the case that an outside observer has something unique to bring to the study of a society, it is also the case that an insider, too, has advantages. What is needed here is more collaborative and exploratory work, more discussion on the study in hand between anthropologist and people. Of course, to introduce such an element greatly complicates the study itself, but it is the only way, ultimately, to make anthropology active as well as reflective. Examination of this potential field also shows an arena richly filled with irony.

One such example of irony is that the distinction between applied and pure research cannot be upheld in any absolute sense. Here the example is from the use of Malinowski's work. After Papua New Guinea became independent in 1975 the first prime minister, Michael Somare, received a deputation of Trobrianders bearing with them a copy of one of Malinowski's books. This showed incontrovertibly, they said, that their rivals of the Kabisawali Association were impostors and their own sub-clan was that of preeminent rank. The irony here is that since Malinowski anthropologists had attacked his account of the paramount chief of Omarakana, the village where he lived, arguing that the system was more egalitarian than Malinowski (and his hosts) had allowed (Somare 1975; Uberoi 1962).

Second, when local scholars are faced with anthropologists' explanations, they sometimes provide simpler—and in that sense perhaps more scientific—ones. The distinguished American anthropologist George Murdock, in his Huxley Lecture for 1971, provides a case of this. Edward Sapir, the anthropological linguist, was once conducting a seminar at Yale on religion, attended by a

Nyoro student from Uganda. The student read a paper in which he mentioned that in his society the shrines of the war god were tended exclusively by priestesses. Sapir proceeded to propound first one and then another alternative theory as to why this might be so, using Freudian theory to explain the apparent paradox. He then triumphantly asked the student which of the two interpretations was right. The student replied: "Neither is correct. The explanation is really quite simple. You see, when war occurs in my country, all the men go out to fight, and no one is left except women to tend the cult of the war god" (Murdock 1971:23). Needless to say, that might not be the last word on the matter, but it is a cautionary tale, which raises the question of the degree of privilege analysis may claim (Murdock 1971).

A third example is a kind of reverse case of the above that was once humorously invented by Rivers. In combating Lucien Levy-Bruhl's theory of prelogical mentality, Rivers pointed out that it is the different arrangement of categories from culture to culture that has led to false suppositions of prelogical thought. He imagines a Melanesian anthropologist sent to study English kin terms:

> He would soon find that we use terms of relationship in a way which to him is hopelessly confused and inexact. In studying the connotation of such terms as uncle and aunt, he would find that we include under these two terms relationships which he distinguishes very carefully. . . . He will return to his home and announce . . . that the English people, in spite of the splendor of their material culture, in many ways show signs of serious mental incapacity. . . . It may even be that . . . he propounds the view that the hyper-development of material culture has led to an atrophy of thought-processes, and suggests as a suitable title for the condition, that of post-logical mentality. (Rivers 1912:401–402)

Was Rivers himself taking a crack here at his materialistic culture under cover of an imagined Melanesian social scientist?

Fourth, and finally, is an example taken from the heart of academia. This is a complaint made against anthropologists by the philosopher Karl Popper in the course of an essay on the logic of the social sciences, first read at the University of Tübingen during a controversy with Theodor Adorno. Popper recounts how he took part in a four-day conference, set up by a theologian, in which philosophers, biologists, anthropologists, and physicists took part. The subject for discussion was science and humanism. After two days, four or five people began to feel that they had raised the discussion "to an uncommonly high level," Popper says. Then the anthropologist spoke, saying that he had come not to listen to what they were talking about but to study their "verbal behavior," since as a result of studying dozens of discussion groups he had learned that the topic discussed is relatively unimportant:

> What interests us is . . . the manner in which one person or another attempts to dominate the group and how his attempts are rejected by the others, either singly or through the formation of a coalition; how after various attempts at this a hierarchical order and thus a group's equilibrium develops and also a group ritual of verbalization. (Adorno et al. 1976:93)

Popper asked the anthropologist whether he had listened to the actual arguments, and the latter replied that he had not, as to do so might cause him to lose his objectivity by becoming involved. Besides, his concern was with the function of such arguments in establishing influence, not with their validity as reasoned statements. Popper protests the behavioristic ideal of objectivity coupled with the oddly contrary position of philosophical relativism supposedly shown by the anthropologist here, and he dismisses it all as absurd. What Popper apparently fails to notice is the humor of the occasion. His outrage at being treated as an object of study should help to explain to us why people elsewhere, too, object to anthropological enquiries. Does he protest, however, a little too much? Elsewhere in the same volume another contributor notes that the very conference Popper was speaking to was indeed dominated in the way the anthropologist claimed!

It should be clear, then, that what we in fact need is a combination of viewpoints from outside and inside, although one should not label these confidently as "objective" and "subjective" respectively. Instead, we should recognize, as I have noted earlier for the discipline of social anthropology as a whole, that they correspond to different interests in and aspects of the phenomena studied. A paradigm for how to combine such aspects was provided long ago by Marcel Mauss in his richly contextual study of the practice of gift giving (Mauss 1954). Mauss was, one might say, a fieldworker's theorist, for he drew his vision of "total" social facts out of a minute and enthusiastic study of ethnographic details. His work testifies both to the buoyancy of data gathered by others and to the creativity of his imagination in working on these. For me, therefore, his essay is an enduring inspiration whose potential can be carried forward as a model for the future rather than simply commemorated as belonging to the past. "The first age was golden," wrote Lévi-Strauss in his dedication page to the first volume of *Structural Anthropology*. Quoting from Hesiod's *Works and Days*, Lévi-Strauss was referring to the school of thinkers inspired by Durkheim, among whom Mauss was prominent. Mauss himself said that fieldwork is like taking a fishing net out to sea: the fish you catch will depend on the net you use and how you use it—that is, on your theory and your methods.

References

Adorno, Theodor, Ralf Dahrendorf, Harald Pilot, Hans Albert, Jürgen Habermas, and Karl R. Popper
    1976 *The Positivistic Dispute in German Sociology*. Translated by G. Adey and D. Frisby. Heinemann, London.
Asad, Talal (editor)
    1973 *Anthropology and the Colonial Encounter*. Ithaca Press, London.
Barth, Fredrik
    1966 *Models of Social Organization*. Royal Anthropological Institute Occasional Paper No. 23. Royal Anthropological Institute, London.
Berlin, Brent, and Paul Kay
    1979 *Basic Color Terms: Their Universality and Evolution*. University of California Press, Berkeley.
Evans-Pritchard, Edward E.
    1940 *The Nuer*. Clarendon Press, Oxford.

1951   *Kinship and Marriage among the Nuer.* Clarendon Press, Oxford.
1956   *Nuer Religion.* Clarendon Press, Oxford.
Fortes, Meyer
1969   *Kinship and the Social Order.* Aldine, Chicago.
Foster, George M., Thayer Scudder, Elizabeth Colson, and Robert V. Kemper (editors)
1979   *Long-term Field Research in Social Anthropology.* Academic Press, London.
Golson, Jack
1982   The Ipomoean Revolution Revisited: Society and the Sweet Potato in the Upper Wahgi Valley. In *Inequality in New Guinea Highlands Societies,* edited by Andrew J. Strathern, pp. 109–136. Cambridge University Press, Cambridge.
Hage, Per, and Frank Harary
1983   *Structural Models in Anthropology.* Cambridge University Press, Cambridge.
Holy, Ladislav
1979   Nuer Politics. *Queen's University of Belfast Papers in Social Anthropology* 4:23–48.
Hymes, Dell (editor)
1969   *Reinventing Anthropology.* Random House, New York.
Jarvie, Ian C.
1964   *The Revolution in Anthropology.* Routledge and Kegan Paul, London.
Kelly, Raymond C.
1985   *The Nuer Conquest.* University of Michigan Press, Ann Arbor.
Kuper, Adam
1980   The Man in the Study and the Man in the Field: Ethnography, Theory and Comparison in Social Anthropology. *European Journal of Sociology* 21:14–39.
Kuper, Adam (editor)
1977   *The Social Anthropology of Radcliffe-Brown.* Routledge and Kegan Paul, London.
Labby, David
1976   *The Demystification of Yap: Dialectics of Culture on a Micronesian Island.* University of Chicago Press, Chicago.
Laracy, Hugh
1976   Malinowski at War, 1914–18. *Mankind* 10(4):264–268.
Leach, Edmund R.
1976   A Natural Science of Society? The Radcliffe-Brown Lecture. *Proceedings of the British Academy* 62. British Academy, London.

Leach, Edmund R., and Jerry W. Leach (editors)
    1983   *The Kula: New Perspectives on Massim Exchange.* Cambridge University Press, Cambridge.
Lévi-Strauss, Claude
    1969   *The Elementary Structures of Kinship.* Translated by James H. Bell and John R. von Sturmer. Beacon Press, Boston.
Malinowski, Bronislaw
    1922   *Argonauts of the Western Pacific.* Routledge and Kegan Paul, London.
    1967   *A Diary in the Strict Sense of the Term.* Translated by Norbert Guterman. Routledge and Kegan Paul, London.
Mauss, Marcel
    1954   *The Gift.* Translated by Ian Cunnison. Cohen and West, London.
Murdock, George P.
    1971   Anthropology's Mythology. *Proceedings of the Royal Anthropological Institute.* Royal Anthropological Institute, London.
Radcliffe-Brown, Alfred R.
    1932   *The Andaman Islanders.* Free Press, Glencoe, N.Y.
Rivers, W. H. R.
    1912   The Primitive Concept of Death. *Hibbert Journal* 10:393–407.
    1922   *History and Ethnology.* Macmillan, New York.
    1924   *Social Organization.* Knopf, New York.
Rosaldo, Michelle
    1980   *Knowledge and Passion: Ilongot Notions of Self and Social Life.* Cambridge University Press, Cambridge.
Sacks, Karen
    1979   Causality and Chance on the Upper Nile. *American Ethnologist* 6(3):437–448.
Sahlins, Marshall D.
    1976   *Culture and Practical Reason.* University of Chicago Press, Chicago.
Schneider, David M.
    1984   *A Critique of the Study of Kinship.* University of Chicago Press, Chicago.
Slobodin, Richard
    1978   *W. H. R. Rivers.* Columbia University Press, New York.
Somare, Michael T.
    1975   *Sana.* Niugini Press, Port Moresby.
Spindler, George D. (editor)
    1970   *Being an Anthropologist.* Holt, Rinehart and Winston, New York.

Strathern, Andrew J.
   1971   *The Rope of Moka*. Cambridge University Press, Cambridge.
   1972   *One Father, One Blood*. Australian National University Press, Canberra.
Strathern, Andrew J. (editor)
   1982   *Inequality in New Guinea Highlands Societies*. Cambridge University Press, Cambridge.
Strauss, Hermann, and Herbert Tischner
   1962   *Die Mi-Kultur der Hagenberg-Stämme*. Cram, de Gruyter, Hamburg.
Uberoi, Jit Singh
   1962   *Politics of the Kula Ring*. Manchester University Press, Manchester.
Vicedom, George F., and Herbert Tischner
   1943–48   *Die Mbowamb*. 3 vols. Friederichsen, de Gruyter, Hamburg.
Weiner, Annette B.
   1976   *Women of Value, Men of Renown: New Perspectives in Trobriand Exchange*. University of Texas Press, Austin.

FOUR

The Limits of Understanding

in Anthropology

1986

One of the prime claims of anthropology is that it enables us to understand "other cultures"—other, that is, than the ones we ourselves have been brought up in prior to becoming anthropologists. To what extent is this claim true? We can make three separate, but connected, approaches to this problem. One is made by distinguishing logically and semantically between different sorts of "understanding." This approach, I think, is necessary to provide the groundwork for the other two, which are to look through ethnographic cases of attempts to reach such understandings and to evaluate them critically and to use material from one's own fieldwork and life experience in order to illuminate more directly suggestions that emerge from discussion of the literature.

The question of what is meant by "understanding" is clearly a philosophical one. The kind of understanding with which I am largely concerned here is akin to the concept of *Verstehen* developed by Wilhelm Dilthey (Dilthey 1976; Weber 1949). Specifically, as a practicing anthropologist, I am concerned with this concept. When we say that we "understand" some feature of a culture we are studying, what sorts of things do we generally mean by making such a claim? It seems to me we are claiming that we can first grasp the feature within its own context and then successfully translate it in such a way that it appears meaningful to us. Ques-

This material for this chapter was first presented as a lecture when I was being interviewed for the position of Mellon Professor of Anthropology at the University of Pittsburgh in February 1986. A version of it was also delivered at the University of Tokyo in September of that year.

tions of translatability and rationality are inevitably involved, as well as the underlying comparability of different cultures (see Augé 1982; Sperber 1985). However, anthropological analysis goes further than this: it purports to be able to explicate other cultures *in their own terms*, and simultaneously to be able to *explain* them by reference to theories essentially drawn from the observer's own cultural and historical milieu. These two aims of understanding and explanation are therefore usually separated. There may also be conflict between them, since "understanding" may be set up as a rival form of explanation to the word "explanation" itself. Regardless of this, both approaches are vulnerable to what may be called "hidden ethnocentrism," in which we think we are applying value-free or objective concepts to our data whereas in fact we are still unconsciously importing ideas of a cultural kind which may or may not be suitable to the task in hand. Coming to terms with this difficulty is an ongoing process in anthropology. Substantive and empirical research methodologies cannot completely guard against it. Rather, over periods of time, self-realizations on the part of the anthropologist can open new areas of comprehension of the culture being studied and thus lead to an increment in understanding. I will give examples of this process, which I take to be fundamental, later.

A point which must be added here is that, if we look for sources through which to underpin our belief that cross-cultural understanding is possible at all, there are only two broad standpoints we can effectively adopt. The first is that there are levels of similarity between cultures and languages that make translation and comparison feasible. One version of this idea appeared early on in the history of anthropological studies as the doctrine of "the psychic unity of mankind." This viewpoint also bridges over to the second approach, that is, the proposition that there are species-level characteristics resulting from the interplay of biological and cultural evolution, and it is possible to identify these characteristics and use them as a yardstick in order to apprehend cultural universals. An important theme here is the nature of the emotions and emotional expressions among different peoples. One discipline that gains some prominence in this context is that of human ethology (Eibl-Eibesfeldt 1984). Theories which fall into line with hypotheses of psychic unity include Lévi-Strauss's version of structuralism with its emphasis on fundamental structures of the mind; Piaget's postulates on the ontological development of logic in the human child; Chomsky's theory of the universal grammar; and Jung's theory of symbolic archetypes. In turn these theories all are placed somewhat in question by those approaches stressing phenomenological "bracketing" of our statements and/or the definite particularities of Geertzian hermeneutics.

Yet all approaches must depend ultimately on some notion of translatability and therefore of commonality, for otherwise different languages and cultures would indeed be, in the striking phrase once employed by Alfred Gell, "windowless monads" (Gell 1980). That they are not so is a part of every anthropologist's experience in the field. Equally, though, that same experience should teach us to beware of thinking that we can easily shuffle off the coils of culture and quickly grasp the object of our study in its entirety. What regularly happens in the struggle to express our findings is that we bend the accepted meaning of terms in our language of communication in order to encompass the senses of words in the language of investigation; or else we give up the struggle and incorporate key words from the culture under study directly into our English discourse. This, for example, is what I did with the Melpa term *moka*, denoting a class of ceremonial exchange transactions of prime importance in Melpa culture (A. J. Strathern 1971). Or we take terms which have a loose meaning in English and give them a more precise significance: this is what was done with "descent," for example, by Rivers, Fortes, and others (Rivers 1924; Fortes 1953). Later, we may find that this precise meaning does not fit well with a further range of cases, and the meaning has to be relaxed again, as when we try to discuss New Guinea Highlands social systems. The process is rather like what Evans-Pritchard described for the refashioning of Nuer genealogies: one of clipping, patching, and telescoping analytical terms as we move across cultures.

Veritably, we move through a mine field. But recognition that it is a mine field is preferable to the simplistic view that we can easily create etically universal concepts and apply these to every instance that comes up. As has often been pointed out, what we think of as etic may turn out to be only emic after all. I have cited the term "descent." More widely, we may instance the huge debates on the meaning of "kinship," with the polarizations between "descent" and "alliance" theorists or the arguments about "genealogy" versus "category." These were the stuff of academic life when I was a student in the 1960s, the material for ardent and acrimonious contention of a quasi-theological type. As such, at one level they were entirely futile. If you begin with an ostensibly etic definition of kinship as this or that and then find that a certain people do or don't classify persons in that way, what you have achieved? Possibly very little, depending on the scope of the initial definition adopted (cf. Schneider 1984). Yet in another sense the debates were quite fundamental: Is there a universal, biologically constrained, substratum of culture, and is this to be found in the domain we index as "kinship"? The debate has reemerged in recent years in arguments between sociobiologists and cultural anthropologists (Kurland 1979). It lurks also in the background of the now almost overexposed contest between Derek Freeman and the ghost of Margaret Mead on Samoan sexual mores (Freeman 1983).

I will take this contest as my first ethnographic "case" here, not because I have anything to add to the substantive war cries, thrusts, parries, groans, whoops, trumpetings, tut-tuttings, and suspirations which have marked it, but because one overall point emerges from it. Whatever the balance of points of detail between Derek Freeman and Margaret Mead (see Bargatzky 1988), it remains true that general characterizations of people in emotive or evaluative terms are fraught with difficulty, and this represents one immediate "limit of understanding" in the discipline of anthropology. Thus, Margaret Mead thought that the young Samoan girls she knew on her first fieldwork had free and easy sex lives and attitudes towards sex, and this became generalized as an attribute of their culture (Mead 1949). Freeman, on the basis of his much more prolonged fieldwork and his own sharper awareness of moral issues, finds that Samoan culture is marked by conflict, guilt, violence, and rebellion, thus controverting Mead's more idyllic picture, and playing Oscar Lewis to Mead's Robert Redfield (see also Gerber 1985). But who is to say in a definitive manner what, in general, the Samoans are like? Perhaps we should blame matters on Ruth Benedict for starting this custom of making an overall assessment of cultures in terms that purport to capture their ethos (Benedict 1934). Samoan commentators themselves do not all agree with either Freeman or Mead on these matters and find it equally irritating to be labeled as carefree savages or as worried puritans. I have often, on parallel lines, reflected on the inappropriateness of characterizing the Mae Enga and the Kuma in the Papua New Guinea Highlands as "prudes" and "lechers" respectively (Meggitt 1964).

The point is that such terms belong to whole complexes of values, feelings, attitudes, and practices, and at best only a small part of such complexes is reflected in the ethnographic reality. At worst, they may be simply wrong, based on inadequate knowledge. For the Mae Enga it appears to be the case that adult men are reluctant to mention such things as female genitals in normal discourse. On the other hand, Mae women are much less inhibited among themselves in their references to males and to sexuality in general. A male ethnographer might not pick this up very readily (Polly Wiessner, personal comment, 1986). Designation of the Kuma as "lechers" seems to have been based simply on the fact that girls were courted by men before their marriage, and sexual intercourse was sometimes permitted as a part of courtship (see O'Hanlon 1989). Conflict enters when Kuma girls are subsequently pushed into marriages with men other than their lovers. Where is the "lechery" in all this?

But to return to the Freeman-Mead debate, Mead's attempt to depict Samoan adolescence was no chance or isolated project. Her aim was quite deliberate, and that was to speak to the people of her own culture about a problem in their social lives through the medium of her ethnography. Specifically, her focus was adolescent rebellion or intergenerational conflict. A "negative" case of this was necessary for her to find her critical "voice" and tell her fellow Americans that their problems were culture-bound and therefore neither ineluctable nor universal. Essentially, then, her "finding," or her "understanding," was set into an already existing gestalt involving the bearers of her home culture just as much as the Samoans. Some version of this gestalt is implied, as I have argued, in all anthropological writings, but the rub here is that the gestalt in this case may have had a retro-effect on Mead's understanding in the field itself. For this reason alone it is important in anthropology at least to begin with the aim of understanding other cultures for the sake of the culture itself and not in order to convey some "loaded" set of messages back to one's own culture.

Freeman's concern is ostensibly quite different. He wants to tell us that adolescent conflict probably *is* universal and does have biological roots located in our phylogenetic history. He may be right, though refutation of Mead's ethnography on Samoa certainly does not establish this point *ipso facto*. It is clear also that considerable ground is still left to the domain of culture since cultures do vary greatly in terms of the extent to which such conflict is emphasized or played down. His own moral or ethical concern is also universalistic: we must be prepared to evaluate other cultures, and biology can serve as one yardstick. So, at bottom, his concern in this respect is homologous with Mead's, only his substantive conclusions are diametrically opposed to hers. Freeman's anthropology, therefore, is just as much a morality as it is a science.

That Mead's concerns were as I have stated them can also be shown by reference to some of her other work carried out in Papua New Guinea. Her three Sepik studies provide the classic locus here. Based on her field tours with the Mundugumor, Arapesh, and Tchambuli (Chambri), Mead delineated three different gender stereotypes, only one corresponding to popular American views of the time. Thus, among the Mundugumor, males were aggressive and females passive (thus equaling the Western stereotype); among the Tchambuli, men were "effeminate" and artistic while women were strong and aggressive traders; while among the Mountain Arapesh both sexes were mild mannered (Mead 1935). Mead's purpose again was to tell her fellow Americans that gender relations are culturally variable. Deborah Gewertz's subsequent study on the Chambri makes it clear that they may also be historically variable within the one culture (Gewertz 1983). Many scholars have wondered, though, whether in Mead's zeal to make her point she may not have forced her ethnographic evidence beyond what it can really bear. Her erstwhile husband Reo Fortune's account of Arapesh warfare certainly suggested that there was a violent as well as a gentle side to behavior among the Mountain

Arapesh with whom they both worked (Fortune 1939). The tendency to generalize in such a way as to say something worthy of publicity which shows up in Mead's work may also have been one factor to which students at the University of Papua New Guinea responded aggressively when they attended Mead's public lectures given there on her occasional visits during the 1970s. Mead had her own way of putting these students down. Once, when a Manus student challenged her ethnography, she said, "I got this from your grandparents. That is why I know it and you don't." In another case she told John Kasaipwalova, a notable Trobriand writer, that he wouldn't have known he had a culture if she had not told him so. Reviewing, then, the Freeman-Mead controversy in terms of my theme, I conclude that their "understandings" were as much located within their own cultures and backgrounds as among the Samoans. And this fact also indicates a limit: they write about Samoan culture largely to prove a point whose relevance is located outside of the Samoan culture itself. Freeman's views are in my opinion by far the more persuasive; but that does not alter the conclusion here.

My second and third examples, also drawn from Melanesia, are rather less heavily weighted with emotive undertones, and remove us from morality and ethology into the world of structuralism. I will take up discussions between ethnographers on closely related peoples whom they have studied, first between Epeli Hau'ofa and Mark Mosko on the Central and Bush Mekeo people of Papua and then between Bernard Juillerat and Alfred Gell on Yafar and Umeda villagers in the West Sepik (or Sandaun) Province.

Epeli Hau'ofa is from a Tongan missionary family transplanted into Papua New Guinea. He grew up in his adopted country, and on deciding to become an anthropologist he first tutored at the University of Papua New Guinea. He then carried out fieldwork from the Australian National University in Beipa'a village among the Central Mekeo during 1969–73. Mark Mosko is an American scholar who worked for twenty-six months (1974–76) among the Bush Mekeo, a small congeries of tribes numbering in all 1,841 persons in 1970 and living to the northwest of the Central Mekeo, whose population Hau'ofa calculates to have been 6,411 in 1971 (Hau'ofa 1981:28; Mosko 1985:15). The general presentation of ethnography by these two authors makes it clear that they are indeed talking about closely related cultures, although it is difficult to arrive at a clear index of this situation. Hau'ofa calls the Bush Mekeo "Kaopo," a Central Mekeo term meaning "swamp people," and seems to separate them from the "real Mekeo," whom he studied; but Mosko identifies a number of terms as cognates in the respective languages, and in his concluding remarks clearly thinks that his model for analysis of Bush Mekeo cultural categories provides also a basis for criticizing or reinterpreting Hau'ofa's own materials (Mosko 1985:129; Hau'ofa 1981:11). Noting that this is something we cannot be too sure about, we can still pay attention to the terms of Mosko's criticism. Mosko claims that his understanding of ethnography is better than Hau'ofa's because it is constructed rigorously in terms of the Bush Mekeo's own categories and does not import into these the generalized idea of status inequality versus equality such as Hau'ofa employs.

> To an English-speaking outsider, relations of senior and junior siblings and clans, of wife-giver and wife-receiver, and of chief, sorcerer, and commoner etc. all seem to involve variations of political "inequality." This supposed uniformity, however, does not have any clear counterpart in indigenous understandings. . . . There is no single category opposition such as "equal" versus "unequal" applicable to all of these contexts. . . . In his enthusiasm to articulate the elements of Mekeo society to the single ideal of "inequality" Hau'ofa has inadvertently distorted the very character of the categories and relations he is investigating." (1985:240–241)

I read this statement at first with a feeling of resistance. Hau'ofa's book is a fine piece of work marked by great sensitivity to Mekeo culture. He does not bring any single encompassing approach such as structuralism to his data, as Mosko himself does (and structuralism was certainly not invented by the Bush Mekeo as one of their cultural categories). However, it does seem that Mosko has an important point here. He is challenging the validity of what is essentially a sociological concept such as "inequality" as it is applied descriptively to a range of Mekeo social relations. The

first basis of his challenge is that apparently this is not a translation term, it does not correspond to Mekeo ethnosociology. This is
worth noting, but is not in itself necessarily definitive. The second
part of his challenge, though, is to say that inequalities are sometimes reversed and that his quadripartite scheme of structural oppositions plus their inversions can handle this state of affairs more
neatly than Hau'ofa's concepts of "inequality" and "ambivalence."
His work is thus essentially a systematization of Hau'ofa's, em-
ploying many of the same binary oppositions which Hau'ofa also
identified, but setting these into quadripartite structures through
which, for example, relations of inequality are inverted and thus
become ones of equality in a manner reminiscent of the "alternating disequilibrium" I proposed as a basic pattern of the Hagen
moka (A. J. Strathern 1971).

There is irony in this situation. Hau'ofa was one of the first of
the "indigenous anthropologists" in the Pacific. On the basis of his
experience as a lecturer at the University of Papua New Guinea, he
wrote an article in which he criticized the type of characterization
Sahlins once made of the Melanesian big-man as leader, comparing him implicitly to a freebooting capitalist entrepreneur (Sahlins
1963; Hau'ofa 1975). Hau'ofa also pointed out that because
Melanesian societies usually lack developed forms of chieftainship
they are somehow treated as being more "primitive" or lower on
the evolutionary scale than Polynesian societies by anthropologists
who classify them in this way (see Thomas 1989). As a Polynesian
brought up in Melanesia, and as an anthropologist, Hau'ofa
clearly fought hard to achieve a more balanced and internally
based view than some others had conveyed before him. However,
as it happened, his study of the Mekeo landed him among a people who do have a well-developed form of chiefship and whose ritualized social behavior is at least comparable to that of the chiefly
societies in Polynesia. Hence, perhaps, the emphasis on social inequality in his book. Mosko, not having any particular relevant
cultural background for his study but armed only with the tenets
of structuralism, finds that Hau'ofa's categories need to be embedded more deeply into Mekeo categories themselves, and he notes
that inequality relations can be reversed. One can, I think, cau-
tiously nod towards this emendation and improvement in under-

standing. At the same time it is surely worth noting also that Central Mekeo live in larger villages than Bush Mekeo. Beipa'a, a village where Hau'ofa lived, had a population of 1,000 and was the largest of all Mekeo villages. Might it not be that hierarchy was more greatly marked in those circumstances, perhaps accompanied by a stronger productive economy than the Bush Mekeo have? A materialist viewpoint injected into this interpretive debate might enable us to comprehend and explain the apparent differences observed by the ethnographers.

My review of the Mosko-Hau'ofa issue, then, indicates that while both authors depend on some introduction of outside schemes of thought (in Hau'ofa's case the sociology of inequality, in Mosko's Lévi-Straussian structuralism), Mosko has probably introduced an important refinement into the analysis. At the same time his approach does not preclude us from attempting further sociological comparisons between the two populations. Again, this debate can be paralleled in the disagreements between Daryl Feil and Mervyn Meggitt on the operation of the Enga *tee* exchange system in the highlands. Briefly, Meggitt has argued for a "group" and "male" oriented focus in analyzing the *tee*, and Feil for an "individual" and "female" one. Each may be right, for the central and fringe Enga areas respectively (Meggitt 1974; Feil 1984).

In Mosko's approach, a good deal of emphasis is laid on exegesis by informants. This is what at least started him on his road of interpretation, he says. It is a point to which I warm, and it brings me to my next pair of writers, Gell and Juillerat. The quadripartite structure which motivates my treatment here could be expressed as : Hau'ofa : Mosko : Gell : Juillerat. Earlier I quoted Gell's phrase "windowless monads," coined as part of his response to a criticism by Juillerat of his work "Metamorphosis of the Cassowaries" (Gell 1975). Gell's position in this reply was that in his book he had used sociological ideas found in the writings of people such as Edmund Leach (but surely also Lévi-Strauss) to illuminate the Umeda ritual system centered on the Ida fertility cult; and without the use of general ideas of this sort single cultures might be described, but no comparisons between them can be made. Juillerat, on the other hand, stresses the need for more intensive fieldwork and for an understanding of indigenous exegesis. Referring back quickly to Mosko's work, we can see that in his treatment such exegesis certainly does *not* preclude comparisons. He uses it to build his quadripartite models and then shows how a similar approach can be used on Trobriands and Tikopia ethnography. Juillerat is less ambitious. He wishes simply to correct Gell's argument that there is no native exegesis. There is, he says, but it is secret, and perhaps that is why Gell did not discover it. The same may perhaps be true for Fredrik Barth's denial of exegesis among the Baktaman. Compare, at any rate, his claim with Poole's lengthy display of exegesis among the Bimin Kuskusmin. This revelation by Juillerat also has an impact on Brunton's earlier criticism of Gell. It is not that the religion is incoherent, but that its coherence is hidden from outsiders and sometimes insiders as well (Gell 1975, 1980; Juillerat 1986; Barth 1975; Poole 1976; Brunton 1980; Wagner 1984).

Let us look briefly at some substantive matters between the two authors. What did the exegesis reveal? Basically Juillerat brings forward two points from the myriad of well-researched details. One is that the whole ritual refers back to a secret myth in which primordial male and female deities gave birth to male children as "sons of the blood." This myth is also a cosmic myth in that it gives meaning to Sky and Earth, East and West, and the creation of parts of the natural world out of the body of the Great Mother. The second point is that the ritual, as a creation of "new men," represents a stage in the emancipation of the male child into adulthood, away from the mother, but the stage reached is actually that of aiming at his mother's breast so as to release from it the milk—the *first* act of the suckling child.

The symbolism is complex and overloaded but returns endlessly to the themes of male and female, sago and coconut palm, semen and blood, the central versus the lateral, black and polychrome colors. Much of this was actually guessed by Gell or arrived at by other means. However, the cassowary symbolism, which Gell makes a focus of his analysis—and the title of his book—emerges as not tied distinctly to the *eli* or *eri* figures, the black-painted dancers who open the sequence, but rather as pervasive throughout the entire ritual. There is no real evidence from the Yafar fieldwork that the sequence does represent uniquely a metamorphosis of the cassowaries, or that "cassowary" means "man." Rather, to the contrary, in the primal myth it seems likely that the Great Mother was a cassowary and when she died in childbirth her husband cut off her breast and placed it in the sky as the sun. When at the close of the ritual the red bowmen shoot their arrows, it is at the sun, or the mother's breast, that they aim. A hit on their target will split the breast and release its milk, that is, cause the sun to shine (Juillerat 1986, 1992).

Juillerat's information on these points came from a few men only. The names of the primal human pair in the myth are secret, and he gives only the first letters of these names. Most of the participants and spectators do not know the details of the myths, yet together the rituals, spells, stories, and songs participate in a general set of representations. Juillerat himself goes further and sees the details given to him as tantamount to laying a trail for psychoanalytical interpretation of the whole ritual. The ritual, he says, enacts both the quasi-incestuous relationship of son to mother and the son's emancipation and growth towards society guided by his mother's brother. The potentially punitive father is absent.

It is not the case, then, that attention to exegesis precludes further interpretation. But it may lead to a different kind of interpretation from that otherwise envisaged. Gell himself saw that there may be an Oedipal element in the Ida, but his major predilection was towards Lévi-Strauss rather than Freud. Juillerat, while confirming the general nature/culture orientation of the ritual, finds that this can be combined with psychoanalytic insights— just as Freud himself saw the establishment of the incest taboo as the beginnings of ordered society and indeed Lévi-Strauss did in his first major book on elementary structures of kinship (Lévi-Strauss 1949).

Juillerat's general comments on the differences between his approach and Gell's are also a sufficient rebuke to Brunton. He points out that the actors may deny exegesis in order to dissimulate the secret ritual background, and we should not be taken in by this to believe that in fact there is no underlying cosmology. This is an important warning, and one which is particularly apt here. This should not be taken as a rebuke to Gell, however. I well remember how Juillerat first indicated to me that there is indeed an exegetical tradition on the Ida. We were on the Paris Metro, and his brief summary of the primal myth was lost amid the background noise, but I did hear him complimenting Gell on his intuitive powers of getting to the heart of the ritual *even without* explanations by the actors. There we have it. I, too, have the feeling that a great deal of the understanding we achieve is of this creative type, involving a leap into what is unknown, rather like the release of the bowman's arrow into the sky in the Ida itself.

My paired oppositions between ethnographers are not designed to declare "winners" but to point out the issues on all sides. In this case, the following emerges: exegesis definitely increases understanding and leads one of the ethnographers to proceed much further with a passing suggestion made by the other. It definitely does not lead just to an inward-focused account, but suggests parallels also with neighboring cultures (for example, the "cassowary as mother" theme in the wider Sepik area). But at the moment of converting the data thus gained into a psychoanalytic frame it must be recognized that a radically new step has been taken, and it remains moot whether this does or does not enhance the understanding or can function as an explanation of the ritual. For another use of Freudian ideas to explain New Guinea custom, see Gillian Gillison's work on the Gimi of the Eastern Highlands. Gillison offers a Freudian explanation of Gimi female mortuary cannibalism as a return to the mother of the body stuff which proceeds from her in the first place (Gillison 1983).

The overall conclusion from my cases here is remarkably simple: deeper and longer fieldwork with better language control and greater attention to indigenous categories pays off with increments of understanding, but this neither precludes nor automatically leads to the development of further interpretations or theories. In my view, those theories proceed always from some realm of the observer's own culture, and his or her application to ethnography becomes a test of the possibility of interpreting one culture by means of the ideas produced by another. This applies to Marxism, structuralism, functionalism, interpretivism, postmodernism, or whatever theory we have in mind.

The third realm of understanding, about which so far I have said little, is the realm of understanding by experience. Most anthropological fieldwork is conducted through "participant observation," a time-honored phrase covering a multitude of degrees of involvement with the object of study. Since early examples, such as Elizabeth Bowen's *Return to Laughter* (1954), a quite formidable array of books has appeared detailing the anthropologists' personal reactions to and actions in the field. Each of these studies shows clearly that the anthropologist's *feelings* were engaged in crucial ways during the work, often in situations where there was a conflict between the aim of observation and the humanistic wish to help others—classically, in situations of sickness (Mitchell 1987:115–118). Despite this obvious and altogether salient point, there has been little systematic use of these experiences to explore ways in which emotions are experienced or handled differently in the different cultures studied. But it is precisely here, where the sensibilities of both anthropologist and people are engaged at a heightened level, that we find the possibility of grasping the extent to which the feelings we have are culturally bound or shared among certain cultures or perhaps universal (see Lutz 1985, 1988).

I consider that there is indeed a species-specific level of behavior patterns and predispositions based upon our phylogenetic history, and that this level feeds into every culturally defined situation with variable strength according to the power of the cultural definitions themselves and their degree of congruence or otherwise with that species-specific level. To say this is an elaborate way of telling us not very much, but for good reason: accepting the reality of both biology and culture we are then free to observe or hypothesize about their interaction. What we call in ordinary discourse "the emotions" are already cultural artifacts, laden with values and attitudes—one of the most obvious examples being the term "love"—but they are never entirely divorced or emancipated from the biological level either (see Eibl-Eibesfeldt 1988).

In the Highlands societies of Papua New Guinea, these culturally recognized "emotions" are further constrained by the principle of reciprocity that pervades every sphere of life. This principle is used to justify all kinds of conduct in conjunction with three leading modalities of feeling, indexed in the Melpa language, for example, as *popokl*, *pipil*, and *kond*. We may gloss these as "anger," "shame," and "pity," but these glosses are not in themselves particularly illuminating. These are all reactive feelings which are supposed to emerge in response to triggering situations. Individuals are expected to act in accordance with these emotions or feelings in such a way as to recover a balance lost by the intervention of the feeling itself (cf. Schieffelin 1976, on the Kaluli). That is how reciprocity enters. And it is not expected that this process will be overridden by any other rule or higher moral principle or by the supposed closeness of the relationship involved. Thus, if you experience *popokl* as a result of something painful you think has been caused, intentionally or otherwise, by an associate, even a spouse or a sibling, you will take retaliatory action. Of course, in such contests the justice of the actions involved cannot be measured easily, and discussions on forms of compensation or peace making are therefore not always simple. This is most tellingly so in the sphere of close interpersonal relations. Nor are these contexts free from manipulation. The same person may express retaliatory *popokl* one day and criticize a spouse the next day for doing the same. When a spouse is left relatively powerless over a series of conflicts of this kind, suicide may result, and this is to be seen as samsonic, carried out in *popokl* in order to give trouble to the surviving partner and perhaps to haunt him—for almost invariably it is the wife who kills herself. "Anger" and "shame" are the invariable feelings associated with husband-wife conflict, in fact, and often have to do with a background of polygyny and the frustrations and jealousies that accompany it. For example, a man asks a number of women coming out of church after a service for smokes. One of his wives, whom he neglects somewhat, overhears this and challenges him, asking why he has to ask all these women for cigarettes when he himself runs a business selling fried pancakes and therefore has money in his house with which to buy things for himself. Her remarks shame him, and feeling angry he clouts her on the ear, asking her why she has to pursue him and nag him in this way. His shame and anger are communicated to her. She takes a stick and wounds his head. Each then claims compensation in wealth goods from the other. The "Peace Officer" who hears their case tells them they are already quits, as a result of their mutually inflicted injuries which cancel out each other. Neither is satisfied with his pronouncement since each is using the dispute not to end but to further the quarrel and to gain an advantage in inflicting further shame.

The only possible counter to such an escalating process is *kond*, to be "sorry" for the other, and this in itself can imply a kind of superiority that the other party finds irksome instead of comforting. Material payments cannot always contain these negative spirals of feeling, and unless they are checked they are likely to lead to more serious quarrels and a break-up of the relationship. Perhaps it is for this reason that the elimination of *popokl* becomes a major concern within the framework of introduced religion. The "removal" of *bel hevi* (the Pidgin equivalent of *popokl* or "anger") is constantly sought in prayer, worship, and forms of reconciliation within at least the charismatic sects of Christianity. Here the new religion appears to offer a potential way out of an impasse in emotional life which is almost certainly aggravated by modern social conditions. At the same time, emancipation from *bel hevi* is taken as the mark of being a successful Christian, an ideal state that is rarely achieved.

What is at issue in many conflicts is the relative standing of the participants. In this society people are both quick to claim and to deny any claim to relative superiority. Their behavior, guided as it is by the three feeling complexes I have outlined, is quite amenable to analysis in human ethological terms also and is therefore referable to the species-level. What links the general to the particular here is the principle of reciprocity. Specifically, *popokl* corresponds to the dimension of aggression in dyadic relationships, and *kond* to that of appeasement, while *pipil* functions as a means of transition between the other two. If A expresses *popokl* towards B, B may experience *pipil* and then both may express *kond* towards each other, canceling out two negatives with a single reciprocal positive feeling. The particular form that this and other related sequences in Melpa interaction take is at once distinctive of the Melpa themselves and at the same time in line with the general theory of aggression and appeasement developed by ethologists (Eibl-Eibesfeldt 1988).

The claim of equality is carried rigorously into the battle between the sexes also. Throughout the Highlands males claim dominance over females in certain situations. But Mosko's stricture should be remembered here. Such dominance need not extend to *all* situations, and in many contexts of private interaction between spouses, for example, there is no passive acceptance of subordination nor any willingness to sacrifice elements of personal independence to the needs of the other partner. Many actions are taken for granted as if they were part of an existing division of labor, and sentiments of gratitude, sacrifice, or "putting oneself out" for the other are scarcely expressed. I attribute this to a carry-over from the set patterns of traditional life, even though this life and its values no longer may be played out properly between the partners. Women use the new situation to expect more from their husbands when they are giving less back; husbands do the same. The results can be painful. Another matter that is striking is the refusal of spouses to learn things from each other. Attempts by one to "teach" something to the other are resisted stubbornly on grounds that now they are "man-woman" and this form of interaction between them is unacceptable. This notion is by no means peculiar to Melpa culture, and it seems to assert the essential equality created by the sexual bond, regardless of men's claims to the contrary. Significantly, it is wives who mostly resist husbands' attempts to "teach" them anything. In other words, their stand is in resistance to male claims of dominance or superiority in the domestic sphere. Needless to say, learning patterns of response—voice modulation, facial control, expression, and the like—to suit these normally unspoken ideas is not a simple matter for the actors. Even the observer, after years of knowing a culture from the public viewpoint, still lacks a secure basis for interpreting interaction at a continuous personal level, and the observer's "understanding" passes from one difficulty to another until he or she at least achieves a sufficient measure of knowledge to come to grips with the situation. Reaching toward this level of knowledge has over the years propelled me into circumstances in which almost my whole life has been coterminous with "the field," requiring a large measure of disengagement subsequently if only to formulate the understandings I have reached or need to reach.

The field experience I have assembled over the last twenty-two years is comparable to the span of adult life of many men who are now leaders in the clan groups of the Kawelka people with whom I have worked. I have been concerned with giving some of these people their own voices by recording their life histories, and I have done this for an older leader, Ongka, and a younger one, Ru, with interesting results in terms of the different prevailing attitudes these men project: Ongka goes for glory, Ru for empathy. Here, then, is another tool for reaching understanding: besides one's own experience, the self-presented experience of one's friends. This is not to say that through these self-accounts we somehow reach automatically to a privileged level of ethnographic reality (cf. Gewertz and Errington 1987). Not at all. These are voices and viewpoints to place alongside other evidence (A. J. Strathern 1979). But when it comes to the point of interest I have raised here, the delineation of emotions, they surely do provide documents of particular significance, since they let us see into the feelings of people through their own (translated) words. In Ru's autobiography, for example, we see nicely illustrated the etiquette that lies behind *moka* gifts and good and bad feeling generated through them (Ru 1992). Reading a long "text" of this sort helps us to become involved in the emotional life of the individual, much as reading novels does: indeed, a new tradition of quasi-autobiographical novel writing is now springing up in Papua New Guinea (see Mel and Kagl 1984).

My basic treatment of the emotions here follows one part of the approach advocated by Arthur Epstein in his study of shame in Melanesia. Although Epstein concentrates for the most part on shame itself, he recognizes that it is a complex category, and that to understand its significance in a given culture we must place it alongside other concepts that make up a coherent set of terms:—as I have done by linking the Melpa concepts of "shame," "anger," and "pity." In exploring the deeper and perhaps unconscious meanings of action, Epstein employs a specifically Freudian framework of ideas. From this perspective he is able to suggest, for example, that the practice of gifting large numbers of inedible yams to shame one's enemies in the Goodenough Island ceremony called *abutu* (Young 1971) is a symbolic equivalent of giving them feces. Aggressiveness discharged in jokes on Goodenough seems to show this symbolism quite directly. As he readily admits, Epstein's approach is conjectural, and its persuasiveness depends entirely on whether one accepts Freudian theory as such. The general hypothesis he uses is that society must develop means for the management of intrapsychic conflicts, and that major ceremonies may perform this function by providing an "opportunity for the symbolic discharge" of certain forbidden impulses and wishes (Epstein 1984:49).

Epstein rightly points out that we have few studies of child socialization in Melanesia to rely on in order to follow this hypothesis through (see Herdt 1982). I have, however, one suggestion to make. In Hagen people make *moka*, they say, to avoid "shame" on their own part and to assuage the "anger" of others. This is a kind of ritual reversal of overgifting, giving in order to assuage one's own anger and to shame the recipients (as in *abutu*). In practice both structures may be operative, but the indigenous theory places the functions in a good, or socially acceptable, light. If one sees this, as Epstein says, as an acting out or discharge of intrapsychic conflicts, what does it mean? "Anger" in Hagen is decisively generated at the time of weaning. Breast-feeding is permissive and extended, with a postpartum taboo that lasts from two to three years. Anger therefore is associated first with the loss of the breast, which becomes taboo when the mother resumes intercourse with the father. Shame, likewise, is then associated with any attempt to reclaim the breast once it has become taboo. The breast has to be "given away," so to speak. What I would conjecture, therefore, is that making gifts in *moka* is similarly seen as a suppression of consumption in favor of exchange, another kind of "giving away the breast." Giving thus removes shame, as in the indigenous theory itself. It also assuages anger, because it is the breast which can soothe the anger of the frustrated child. In this context, the crescent shape of the famous Hagen pearl shells that are mounted on boards and given in *moka* may be interpreted as reminiscent of the breast itself, and pigs given alive or cooked as substitutions for the whole human body. This conjecture would still leave us with the problem of accounting for the opposite or inverse meaning of the gift, whereby it is the opponent who is shamed. Perhaps one would refer it, as Epstein does, to the anal phase. In Pangia, in the Southern Highlands, when pigs are killed for presentation to visitors, the killer sometimes says, at the point of clubbing the pig, *ne te moa*, "you get feces," and this is explicitly directed towards enemies. This is certainly a symbolic discharge of the type that Epstein suggests may be present in ceremonies elsewhere.

It is important to note here that the above discussion is not intended to be reductionist. The *moka* is not to be simply or solely "explained" with reference to Freudian theory. Certainly not. Explanation demands a multilevel approach in which many different factors are involved. Epstein, too, is aware of this kind of point. He speaks of "negative feedback" rather than of "causal relations." What he means by this is that intrapsychic conflicts do not "cause" institutions such as the *moka*; however, in them certain tendencies which result from these conflicts may find a concealed form of expression, which in turn helps to manage the tendencies in other spheres of life. Like many social science hypotheses, this contains a large amount of guesswork. It is like a reconstructed skeleton extrapolated from a bone here and a bone there. The usefulness of the hypothesis will depend on how much comparative material from other societies is illuminated by it.

I want to close with a further fieldwork problem, that of investigating two different, though related, cultures. This I have done by working with first the Melpa people of the Western Highlands and then the Wiru of the Southern Highlands Province. The first phase of work with the Melpa was carried out in 1964–65, and I developed a sociological hypothesis on the differences to be expected between societies with *moka*-type exchange and those in which production builds up for massive pig-killings (A. J. Strathern 1969). To this end I sought to work in a pig-killing area, and I found myself among the Wiru in 1967. My publications on this people have been relatively sparse by comparison with the output on the Melpa. This has not been without reason. While the terms of my original hypothesis were certainly by and large confirmed (A. J. Strathern 1978), I found it difficult to *relate* to the Wiru culture as I had done to the Melpa. Matters of empathy and

Table 1: Melpa/Wiru Cultural Contrasts

Activity	People	Group Context	Individual Context
Communication at Festivals	Melpa	Verbal	Non-verbal
	Wiru	Non-verbal	Verbal
Face-painting at Festivals	Melpa	Colors stand for social categories	Designs not loaded with category significance
	Wiru	Colors not loaded with category significance	Designs mark male individuality

self-identification are involved here, but also questions of intellectual grasp. I found it disconcerting that at their pig-kills the Wiru did not make elaborate, ordered, and persuasive speeches as Melpa leaders do at *moka*. Lack of these meant that I found it hard to understand what the pig-kills were all about. It was only much later that I realized that communication at those Wiru festivals can be understood as the inverse of the communication process at the Melpa *moka* (Table 1).

My initial failure to recognize this "quadripartite structure" led to the inability to analyze the meanings of these Wiru festivals. During my fieldwork in 1967, also, I could make little of Wiru decorations. Then in 1977 I began asking once more about face designs in Wiru and suddenly learned that each one of these represents a specific bird and its markings. In Hagen the face designs do not work in this way. The designs do not carry much important meaning; rather, the colors do. I had somehow carried over this painfully won conclusion into the Wiru context, and this had blocked me from seeing that, here again, the Wiru and Melpa codes stand in an opposed relationship. Learning these points does not come from the simple observation of facts, but from slow-brewing "fermentation," as one might put it, and this is to my mind another good reason for long-term and repeated association with one's field areas. The limit of one's ultimate understanding may in a sense simply be one's own active life span. Reaching out to another culture is an asymptotic process never completed, but the lure of completion is there—beautiful fruit—and spurs us on. In that struggle our common species identity is both an advantage, in that it gives us some overall initial basis for understanding, and a handicap, because it is so capable of being refracted into a myriad of different cultural shapes, which must be painstakingly identified and studied in their own terms. And there is no simple transformational rule-set that can enable us to move back and forth between biology and culture.

References

Augé, Marc
    1982   *The Anthropological Circle: Symbol, Function, History.* Cambridge University Press, New York.
Bargatzky, Thomas
    1988   Review of *Quest for the Real Samoa,* by Lowell D. Holmes. *Pacific Studies* 11(3):131–150.
Barth, Fredrik
    1975   *Ritual and Knowledge among the Baktaman of New Guinea.* Yale University Press, New Haven.
Benedict, Ruth
    1934   *Patterns of Culture.* Houghton Mifflin, Boston.
Bowen, Elizabeth
    1954   *Return to Laughter.* Gollancz, London.
Brunton, Ron
    1980   Misconstrued Order in Melanesian Religion. *Man* 15(1):112–128.
Dilthey, Wilhelm
    1976   *Selected Writings.* Edited by H. P. Rickman. Cambridge University Press, Cambridge.

Eibl-Eibesfeldt, Irenäeus

1984 *Die Biologie menschlichen Verhaltens: Grundriss der Humanethologie.* Piper, Munich.

1988 The Biological Foundations of Aesthetics. In *Beauty and the Brain,* edited by Ingo Rentschler, Barbara Hertzberger, and David Epstein, pp. 29–70. Birkhauser Verlag, Basel.

Epstein, Arthur L.

1984 *The Experience of Shame in Melanesia: An Essay in the Anthropology of Affect.* Royal Anthropological Institute Occasional Paper No. 40. Royal Anthropological Institute, London.

Feil, Daryl K.

1984 *Ways of Exchange: The Enga Tee of Papua New Guinea.* University of Queensland Press, St. Lucia.

Fortes, Meyer

1953 The Structure of Unilineal Descent Groups. *American Anthropologist* 55:17–41.

Fortune, Reo F.

1939 Arapesh Warfare. *American Anthropologist* 41:22–41.

Freeman, J. Derek

1983 *Margaret Mead and Samoa: The Making and Unmaking of an Anthropological Myth.* Harvard University Press, Cambridge.

Gell, Alfred

1975 *Metamorphosis of the Cassowaries: Umeda Society, Language and Ritual.* Athlone Press, London.

1980 Order or Disorder in Melanesian Religion? Correspondence in *Man* 15(4):735–737.

Gerber, E. R.

1985 Rage and Obligation: Samoan Emotion in Conflict. In *Person, Self, and Experience: Exploring Pacific Ethnopsychologies,* edited by Geoffrey M. White and John Kirkpatrick, pp. 121–167. University of California Press, Berkeley.

Gewertz, Deborah

1983 *Sepik River Societies: A Historical Ethnography of the Chambri and Their Neighbors.* Yale University Press, New Haven.

Gewertz, Deborah, and Frederick Errington

1987 Of Unfinished Dialogues and Paper Pigs. *American Ethnologist* 14(2):367–377.

Gillison, Gillian

1983 Cannibalism among Women in the Eastern Highlands of Papua New Guinea. In *The Ethnography of Cannibalism,* edited by Paula Brown and Donald Tuzin. Society for Psychological Anthropology, Washington, D.C.

Hau'ofa, Epeli
  1975 Anthropology and Pacific Islanders. *Oceania* 45:283–290.
  1981 *Mekeo: Inequality and Ambivalence in a Village Society.* Australian National University Press, Canberra.
Herdt, Gilbert (editor)
  1982 *Rituals of Manhood: Male Initiation in Papua New Guinea.* University of California Press, Berkeley.
Juillerat, Bernard
  1986 *Less Enfants du Sang: société, reproduction et imaginaire en Nouvelle-Guinée.* Editions de la Maison des Sciences de l'Homme, Paris.
Juillerat, Bernard (editor)
  1992 *Shooting the Sun.* Smithsonian Institution Press, Washington, D.C.
Kurland, Jeffrey A.
  1979 Paternity, Mother's Brother, and Human Sociality. In *Evolutionary Biology and Human Social Behavior: An Anthropological Perspective,* edited by Napoleon A. Chagnon and William G. Irons, pp. 145–180. Duxbury Press, North Scituate, Mass.
Lévi-Strauss, Claude
  1949 *The Elementary Structures of Kinship.* Translated by James Bell and John Richard von Sturmer. Beacon Press, Boston.
Lutz, Catherine
  1985 Ethnopsychology Compared to What? Explaining Behavior and Consciousness among the Ifaluk. In *Person, Self and Experience,* edited by Geoffrey White and John Kirkpatrick. University of California Press, Berkeley.
  1988 *Unnatural Emotions.* University of Chicago Press, Chicago.
Mead, Margaret
  1928 *Coming of Age in Samoa.* 1949 ed., New American Library, New York.
  1935 *Sex and Temperament in Three Primitive Societies.* W. W. Morrow, New York.
Meggitt, Mervyn J.
  1964 Male-Female Relations in the Highlands of Australian New Guinea. *American Anthropologist* Special Issue: *New Guinea: The Central Highlands* 66 (4, pt.2):204–224.
  1974 Pigs Are Our Hearts. *Oceania* 44:154–203.
Mel, Michael Y., and Toby W. Kagl
  1984 *Two Highland Novels from Papua New Guinea.* Edited by Andrew J. Strathern. Institute of Papua New Guinea Studies, Port Moresby.
Mitchell, William
  1987 *The Bamboo Fire.* Waveland Press, Prospect Heights, Ill.

Mosko, Mark

1985   *Quadripartite Structures: Categories, Relations, and Homologies in Bush Mekeo Culture.* Cambridge University Press, Cambridge.

O'Hanlon, Michael

1989   *Reading the Skin.* British Museum Publications, London.

Poole, Fitz John Porter

1976   The Ais Am: An Introduction to Male Initiation Ritual among the Bimin-Kuskusmin of the West Sepik District, Papua New Guinea. Ph.D. diss., Department of Anthropology, Cornell University, Ithaca.

Rivers, W. H. R.

1924   *Kinship and Social Organization.* Knopf, New York.

Ru-Kuntil

1992   *Ru-Kuntil (An Autobiography).* Edited by Andrew J. Strathern. National Research Institute, Port Moresby, Papua New Guinea.

Sahlins, Marshall D.

1963   Poor Man, Rich Man, Big Man, Chief: Political Types in Melanesia and Polynesia. *Comparative Studies in Society and History* 5:285–300.

Schieffelin, Edward L.

1976   *The Sorrow of the Lonely and the Burning of the Dancers.* St. Martin's Press, New York.

Schneider, David M.

1984   *A Critique of the Study of Kinship.* University of Michigan Press, Ann Arbor.

Sperber, Dan

1975   *Rethinking Symbolism.* Translated by Alice Morton. Cambridge University Press, Cambridge.

1985   *On Anthropological Knowledge.* Cambridge University Press, Cambridge.

Strathern, Andrew J.

1969   Finance and Production: Two Strategies in New Guinea Highland Exchange Systems. *Oceania* 40:42–67.

1971   *The Rope of Moka: Big-Men and Ceremonial Exchange in Mount Hagen, New Guinea.* Cambridge University Press, Cambridge.

1978   Finance and Production Revisited: In Pursuit of a Comparison. *Research in Economic Anthropology* 1:73–104.

1979   *Ongka.* Gerald Duckworth, London.

Thomas, Nicholas

1989   The Force of Ethnology: Origins and Significance of the Melanesia/Polynesia Division. *Current Anthropology* 30(1):27–41.

Wagner, Roy
    1984   Ritual as Communication: Order, Meaning, and Secrecy in Melanesian Initiation Rites. In *Annual Review of Anthropology,* edited by Bernard J. Siegel, Alan R. Beals, and Stephen A. Tyler, 13:143–155. Annual Reviews Inc., Palo Alto.

Weber, Max
    1949   *The Methodology of the Social Sciences.* Translated and edited by E. A. Shils and H. A. Finch. Free Press, Glencoe, N.Y.

Young, Michael
    1971   *Fighting with Food.* Cambridge University Press, Cambridge.

Emics, Etics, and Systemics:

Theoretical Kicks and Pitches

in Anthropology

1989

My title for this chapter is designed to convey no more than a gentle irony. Just as one reviewer has described my brief forays into theory in the book *A Line of Power* (1984) as "somewhat avuncular," so here I intend to convey a skeptical but friendly interest in what is happening in some of the currently contested arenas of anthropology. Endlessly caught between a dichotomy of "the humanities" and "the sciences," anthropology is surely fated to produce such lengthy duels. By reason of the very dichotomy itself, the arguments are not likely to be resolved once and for all. At most they may issue in a repeated state of "alternating disequilibrium," a phrase I originally invented to describe the outcome of sequences of competitive gift-making in the *moka* exchanges of the Mount Hagen people in Papua New Guinea (A. J. Strathern 1971).

Versions of this dichotomy abound: interpretation versus explanation, qualitative versus quantitative, ethnography versus anthropology—these are some of the pairs that have been used. One way or another, the pairs tend to fit with the emics/etics distinction, which emerged originally out of descriptive linguistics. As we have tended to use this distinction, it has lost the precise meaning it first had: etic renderings were those which took account of

The material for this chapter was written in 1987 but not presented until February 1989 in the visiting speaker's colloquium series at the University of Wisconsin-Madison.

features defined by a grid of characteristics indexing positions of articulation, such that all observable patterns could be pinpointed. Emic renderings were those that established, equally scientifically, those sound differences relevant for semantic purposes. Both etic and emic versions were thus scientific, and both were in a sense observers' constructs. However, etics provided a universal, emics a particular, result: hence the extended sense of this dichotomy in anthropology. But, again, in linguistics, the two are not at odds: phonetics yields a narrow, phonemics a broad, transcription. Until one knows the emics, one transcribes etically and works towards the emic. Etics are in this regard a step towards emics, not a privileged or superior level of discourse. But for objective typological comparisons the etic grid has to be invoked. So with anthropological ethnographies emics are said to yield the local, particular. To make comparisons we require etics. Yet "emes" can be compared directly, perhaps, without translating back into etic forms, or if we do so translate we in fact compare three emic versions, setting up one, in our own language, as the supposedly etic.

However unjustifiably, the emics/etics contrast has come into alignment with the categories of interpretation/explanation and humanism/science. The problem is, of course, that emic assumptions may be smuggled back into an assertedly etic scheme, thus collapsing the dichotomy back on the emic side, with the possibility that there are no etics. I identify this as one of the two great over-hasty tendencies in our subject, that is, the building of prior answers into the questions we ask by insertion of cultural schemata of our own. The other tendency is to imagine that the only way we can make anthropology into a science is by turning it into something else, preferably biology or psychology, both sciences that would reduce the subject matter of propositions in anthropology to their own respective levels of reference. I am not trying to decide the issues in advance here. It may be that these tendencies are in fact correct. But I see them as products of anthropology's actual in-between status and as reactions against this. Both attempt to make anthropology fall into the scientific side of the dichotomy. The first does this by converting it actually into a humanism and then calling this science. The second does it by reaction against the first: since there is a danger of relapsing into humanism, let us avoid this by abandoning entirely the anthropological level and going to levels at which "culture" and "consciousness" are not so awkwardly intrusive or at least where they can be handled experimentally and referred to the human material organism.

My original background in anthropology is from British social anthropology of the 1960s. It is commonplace to observe that the British of this time, bent on creating their own version of anthropology as a science, tended to neglect questions of culture and more specifically excluded psychology from their purview. American anthropologists, if anything, reversed this: they were so concerned with culture and psychology that they created a theory of culture and personality that largely assumed social relations were explanatory factors but did not by itself account for these relations. I was never myself aware of any great taboo in Britain on the discussion of "psychology." Max Gluckman's theories of conflict actually seemed to depend on certain psychological propositions, for example. But I was aware of two distinctions I still consider to be of some importance: the distinction between public and private contexts and between conscious and unconscious meanings. Generally speaking, I learned in my undergraduate days that one could not infer private meanings from public contexts, nor vice versa. Edmund Leach, in particular, pointed this out in his observations on Kachin rituals (Leach 1954). He was equally skeptical about the Durkheimian interpretation relating rituals to social solidarity, and by this he also implicitly countered other psychological propositions. This leaves open, however, the question of whether there *can* be some carryover between these two levels, and without any communication between such levels it becomes hard to know how public meanings are originally created at all (see Obeyesekere 1981). However, in turn, this does not mean that we can at once invoke the unconscious as the source of private meanings. The problem with "the unconscious" is that it also is an emic construct, embedded in a specific discourse. When Freud and Lévi-Strauss tell us about their different versions of what goes on in this unconscious, how do we objectively distinguish their contributions from the myths of those whose constructs they claim to translate and explain? Only, I suggest, by privilege. Freud and Lévi-Strauss are "great minds," hence we must respect them more than the "primitives" about whom they generalize. But is this justified?

In this kind of debate, the work of Meyer Fortes emerges as a crossing station. He builds Freudian metaphors into his account of the Tallensi religion in a way that suggests that the Tallensi might themselves be co-creators of Freudian theory. Robin Horton has taken pains to disentangle these carefully interwoven threads and to insist that we distinguish between Freud's theories and the Tallensi's own ethnopsychology (Fortes 1987; Horton and Finnegan 1973). Much more recently, anthropologists working in the Pacific have examined a range of such ethnopsychologies and called into question whether Western psychological theory is to be seen as explanatory of these or on a par with them. Thus Catherine Lutz's question: "Ethnopsychology compared to what?" (Lutz 1985, 1988).

These examples indicate that even though the British are said to have ignored culture and psychology, in fact both Leach and Fortes raised some fundamental questions on these topics, but without settling them. Generally, though, both were indeed intent on delimiting a special sphere of study for social anthropology as such. It is to the broader and more eclectic domain of American anthropology that we must turn if we want to see the development of a range of theoretical "kicks and pitches" beyond the British framework.

There are many anthropology departments on the North American continent, and they compete for students. This in itself is a stimulus to the production of theories. Currently the old dichotomy is manifesting itself in a heightened version: ultra-Geertzian writers are pitted against biological reductionists, the one set privileging the mind and its labyrinth while the other largely dispenses with it. Ethnographers, meanwhile, get on with their business as usual, using whatever ideas come to hand. Hermeneutics forces us into ever tighter spirals of specificity; sociobiology flattens all into a single drive to maximize fitness. Between such extreme stances there is clearly hardly any meeting ground: the arena is not so much contested as forever divided, and each performer sings to a separate audience. The same process can

occur within departments, becoming a focus for dissent and debate over appointments, courses, programs, and colloquia. While
hermeneutics strains towards a postmodern future, psychoanalysis would take us back into the cultural world of the nineteenth
century, and sociobiology also appears to have strange resonances
with those bullish times of yore.

It is in this context that George Marcus and Michael Fischer
have written their *Anthropology as Cultural Critique*, which attempts
to anchor anthropology in contemporary social process by seeing
it essentially as a *critical* exercise, making comments on society and
raising our social consciousness (Marcus and Fischer 1986). In proposing this idea, they also attempt to reconcile or combine an "interpretive" approach with one derived from political economy.
The time is propitious for such attempts, if they are correct, because Marcus and Fischer see the present as an experimental moment at which major paradigms have broken down and no single
approach has emerged to dominate the scene—a rather exciting
time of eclecticism, growth, and creativity. It is on the whole an
attractive picture, and one which I find congenial, since I must
have been a born eclectic and have in the past suffered because of
this at the hands of gurus and believers. What a relief to discover
that at last I am living in a period that suits me and am not awkwardly out of step with the orthodox wherever I go! The authors
also praise ethnography as being central to the process whereby
anthropology becomes a cultural critique, and this also comforts
me because I have tended to stick with ethnography (albeit oriented towards comparison and hypotheses) to an extent greater
than believers in paradigms consider altogether reputable.

Marcus and Fischer go on to try to chart a course for interpretive
anthropology between obscurantism and vapid overgeneralization, taking into account the conditions of a "shrinking" post-
colonial world in which anthropologists must be more reflexive
and in which people comment back on what the anthropologists
have to say. Once again, I applaud. This is truly how anthropology
looked to me from the perspective of teaching it in Port Moresby,
Papua New Guinea, to descendants of those about whom
Malinowski and Mead had pontificated so freely. Just as the people
about whom we write become more active politically, so we dis-

cover an anthropology that deals not just with culture and personality but with "persons." The point here is that interpretive writing with its emphasis on cross-subjectivity also depends on an objective social change: the creation of a world in which boundaries have been breached. A two-way process occurs: interpretive ethnography absorbs the new world as its context, and theories of political economy need to resituate themselves in a context that recognizes local specificity as well as global patterns. The lesson is in dialectics, and the result is the proliferation of new themes. Michael Meeker's study *Literature and Violence in North Arabia* (1979) is cited tellingly here (Marcus and Fischer 1986:107). Meeker shows that "heroism" became a contested value just when firearms came in and heroism was thus "threatened with obsolescence" (Meeker 1979:152). A similar stage was reached at the end of 1986 in Mount Hagen. By mid-1988 it was possible to see out of the "epistemic murk" (Taussig 1987:132) a new kind of heroism emerging among younger men. The conjunction of an ancient institution, the feud, with a modern instrument, the gun, obviously leads to a rapid perturbation of practice, calling many things into question, just as the emergence of eclecticism does in anthropological theorizing itself.

Marcus and Fischer are, to my mind, strikingly successful in delineating the present state of play in the writing of ethnographies. However, it is also true that the field is littered with the struggling followers of paradigms past. They shrewdly point out that other commentators have tended to concentrate on such dying, resurgent, or nascent paradigm-pushers either to support one paradigm or at least to reconstitute the field in terms of a game between proponents of one or the other major dichotomous divisions. They point out that in the 1960s one of the major contenders was linguistics itself, which supplied us with the emics/etics categorization in the first place. Out of linguistics came, variously, cognitive anthropology (one version of which was ethnoscience), structuralism, and Geertzian symbolic analysis. On these three approaches Marcus and Fischer write:

> Cognitive anthropology's hopes for objective grids came to be seen as just one set of cultural constructions among others. . . .

Structuralism was critiqued . . . as being too distant from the intentionality and experience of social actors, while symbolic analysis . . . was charged with . . . seeing meaning wherever and however the analyst wished. (1986:29)

Their criticisms here are well taken. It is interesting to see that a noted contemporary thinker, Dan Sperber, appears definitely to espouse still the hope that two other disciplines should provide either the model or the solution for problems in anthropological analysis. Sperber makes a distinction between ethnography and anthropology as Marcus and Fischer do, but he is basically condescending about the former. Its task is merely to describe the particular, the culturally variable. Anthropology, on the other hand, has to uncover the universal mechanisms that underlie such particular variations. In criticizing ethnographic analyses, Sperber relies on linguistics as his standard. Concomitantly, in his view anthropology will depend on cognitive psychology for its theory (Sperber 1985). He is inclined to think that the universal mechanisms he seeks may be genetically encoded, although he does not seriously investigate this proposition but merely takes it as being not impossible. His adherence to the linguistic model also leads him to give a strict meaning to the term "meaning" and thereby to deny that symbols "mean" anything in a fixed or codified way. They simply depend on an initially incomplete conceptualization and from this focalize and then further evoke associations. Although Sperber's language is quite different, his ideas are comparable to Victor Turner's notions of "condensation" and "multivocality" of symbols—this despite the fact that he criticizes Turner (Turner 1969). What is entirely missing from the essentially cool, intellectualist, category-oriented approach of Sperber is the "warm-blooded" effect of Turner's analyses: his awareness and delineation of conflict and solidarity and the clash of human values in social process. Instead of this, Sperber's forte is his elegant demonstration of the structurally contrasted properties of, for example, the leopard and the hyena among the Ethiopian Dorze. How true it is, indeed, that ethnographers seem to get the people they deserve; or rather, as we better know, that they construct people after the image of their own thoughts. Yet Sperber can overcome cate-

gories too. In one of his more amusing and less stilted pieces he
admits to having toyed with the idea of hunting a dragon and from
this points out that the boundaries between conceptual worlds are
much more permeable than is often allowed. Phenomenologists
know this. I have often known it, too—as what ethnographer has
not?—discussing in an entirely matter-of-fact way the risks of sorcery to my food supplies or the likelihood that a kinsman has visited someone in a dream. In this example, Sperber becomes both
more truly ethnographic and less rigidly intellectualist than he is
in his other pronouncements. (In passing, we may add that his
ironic mode of writing also signals him as postmodern in one
sense though he is still paradigm-oriented in another.)

Overall, I think that Sperber's very sophisticated, not to say formidable, work nevertheless illustrates very clearly one of the two
tendencies I have identified earlier: he intellectualizes ethnography via the linguistic model, presumably because he feels this is
scientific; and he privileges cognition rather than social process,
replacing anthropology with cognitive psychology. The same im-
pulse leads him to reject semiological interpretation and to reread
Lévi-Strauss so that the master no longer appears to hold a semiological point of view and can be brought into the cognitive fold.
On semiology, Sperber argues that there is no regular correspondence between a symbol and its referent; that exegesis is not an
interpretation but a part of the data to be interpreted; and that unconscious referents may be imputed but cannot be demonstrated.
He concludes that the term "symbol" itself is a "native" term, belonging to some cultures but not others. Thus he reduces it from
an etic or cross-cultural status to a local or emic status. "All keys to
symbols are a part of symbolism itself" (Sperber 1975:50). They become a new object of study from the cognitive viewpoint, but not,
except in passing, from a sociological one. Sperber's mentalistic
approach is thus shown clearly. In the grand French tradition, he
is concerned with knowledge as representation, mental images or
structures, and with how such representations change. The very
objects of our study are thereby defined—not social relationships
but mental entities. And so the walkway to cognition is completed.
Sperber thus stands on the other side, looking back at the concerns
of British social anthropology as though they were futile and had

nothing more to do with his enquiries. A marginal benefit, however, is that Freud's theories are also shown to be faulty. One could add that in Freud's case Sperber's adage applies most forcibly; and moreover, we still require a sociological analysis to show how and why this is so.

Appeals to etically constructed categories, such as cognitive psychology or biology, usually occur when a prior etic category has been recognized as, after all, emic. The search for the etic is always a retreat from the relativism that tends to be implied by immersion in the emic. Like most other anthropologists Sperber has felt the need to discuss relativism, at least partly as a result of reflection on his own experiences in fieldwork. He starts well, with reference to Christopher Crocker's demonstration that the Bororo men know they are making a metaphorical statement when they say "We are red macaws." I have had a similar experience with Hagen men in discussing their concept of the *noman* (which may be glossed as "mind"), an idea which they state is definitely metaphorical. Although the *noman*, like the ancient Greek *thumos*, is supposed to be in the chest, do not expect to find it by cutting someone's chest open! However, worldviews do seem to differ significantly, and not all can be reduced to conscious metaphor, so some place has to be given to relativism. But how much? Sperber points out that if we adopt relativism, we admit that it may be very hard to achieve cross-cultural understanding; nor do we know how different "cognizable worlds" are built up. He goes on to attack the idea of different worldviews, to remind us that "belief" is a slippery concept and that "religious" statements are often distinguished by the speakers themselves from commonsense ones (Sperber 1985:48). He succeeds, therefore, in at least casting doubt on the idea that people actually believe different things; and he then takes off into a linguistic discussion of propositions and representations. What we have called beliefs are actually semi-propositional representations which both people and observer know cannot be checked and hence may be held quite rationally but without certainty—a nice solution for a skeptical anthropologist and a skeptical culture of semi-believers, and a way out of relativism back into cognition. People are not irrational, after all, even by our own demanding Western standards. They are skepti-

cal; almost postmodernists, one might say. Sperber's solution has
the merit of granting sophistication to those we study, and this I
applaud, if only as another useful defense against the totalizing effects of psychoanalytic approaches. But it leaves us in considerable
puzzlement as to what all the big fuss regarding cultural variability has, then, been about and why these cool representations seem
to lead to the spilling of hot blood. Elements of human life are not
so much explained as abolished. Sperber is apparently a universalist, who considers we all think alike, even if we have come to
think remarkably different things. But at least he does not greatly
privilege observer against observed. This is probably because he
eschews the kind of evaluation of different cultures that is the hallmark of two other universalist approaches, the psychoanalytic and
the sociobiological. To these I now turn, by way of the work of
Melford Spiro.

Spiro has long followed a clear Freudian approach. This approach shows in his early work on Burmese supernaturalism, and
it is also followed faithfully by Gananath Obeyeskere in his book
Medusa's Hair (1981). Indeed, it permeates, albeit in a muted form,
the work of many of those who belong to the Department of Anthropology which Spiro founded at La Jolla. One could perhaps
suggest that he is then the instantiation of his own myth-theory—
the dominant father figure. But to the discussion!

In a recent paper Spiro has argued that there are different kinds
of cultural relativism, and that one kind, epistemological relativism, leads to a dead end in anthropology because it reduces our
efforts to ethnographic particularism. Here, I wish to look at his
arguments and suggest places where alternative viewpoints to his
own can be, or should be, constructed. With his main concern, to
show that anthropology can be a scientific subject, I have no disagreement. I am bothered, however, by his insistence that all viewpoints within anthropology other than his own should be labeled
scientifically irresponsible and with some of the moves he makes
in order to arrive at this conclusion. It will be necessary, therefore,
to comb selectively through parts of his argument in order to indicate where my views differ from his.

Spiro's first and basic proposition is that descriptive relativism
is based on the theory of cultural determinism. This he defines as

the idea that "human social and psychological characteristics are produced by culture" (Spiro 1986:259). He does not define culture here, nor does he say which anthropologists have espoused the theory of cultural determinism and in which forms or versions. It is open for us to suggest that this determinism, like relativism in Spiro's formulation, is not one but a number of things, depending on the variant definitions of culture (e.g., mentalist or materialist definitions) used. Spiro chooses a very broad version when he says that human social and psychological characteristics are the contents of culture, which culture is supposed to determine. His definition is convenient for his later discussion of the species-specific evolutionary background to culture: but fits awkwardly with his later list of extra-cultural factors. My comment here is simple. "Cultural determinism" is defined more or less according to what is meant by "culture." Its force varies also according to whether culture is seen in a synchronic or a diachronic way, and whether we are immediately appealing to the concept of discrete whole cultures or merely to the generic idea of "human culture." I find, then, that the basis for the whole ensuing discussion by Spiro is not entirely clear. However, to make his argument work, he needs definitions of the kind he actually has invented.

The next part of the argument has to do with descriptive versus normative relativism, but the issue of normative relativism is not pursued through the body of the paper. Rather, it is left hanging. He distinguishes between trans-cultural and pan-cultural standards by which cultures might be evaluated in terms of their worth. Are there criteria in terms of which cultures could be assigned relative worth on a single scale? Relativists say no. We do not know what Professor Spiro thinks because he does not tell us here. As this is a very big issue, it would have been particularly interesting to have his views. He does say that for relativists all cultures are of equal worth. However, I would reformulate this, because such an assertion would depend on the existence of the very thing relativists are also said to deny, a pan-cultural scale. For true relativists, it would be impossible to say whether one culture is of greater worth than another, because we do not know how to measure worth cross-culturally.

I think this is quite an important point, but it is not Spiro's main concern, so we may pass on to his discussion of cross-cultural forms of logic, where he says that for relativists, "if the logical processes underlying Azande magic violate normal canons of logic, it is nevertheless impermissible to judge it as irrational, because logical canons, like anything else, are culturally variable" (Spiro 1986:261). This is, of course, a *reductio ad absurdum* of the relativist position. There is, however, a better way out of this ethnographic dilemma. This is to say that logical thinking is the same everywhere, but underlying premises about the world vary. The Azande think logically as Westerners do; but their worldview is different. We can also resolve the matter of evaluation by distinguishing between two different meanings of "irrational," one "based on faulty reasoning" and the second "factually incorrect." Zande notions may not be irrational in the first sense but are so in the second, we could argue.

Spiro's real concern is with epistemological relativism, based on what he calls the strong form of descriptive relativism, that which says each culture is unique and incommensurable with others. Once again, I am not sure who said this. Also, I am unsure of the force of "incommensurable." This is not merely a quibble. Must cultures be "commensurable" in order to be compared, for example? What *is* commensurability? Having the same features? Or having features which are transformations of those in another culture? Or what? If there are anthropologists who have held to the view that each culture is unique *and therefore* cannot be compared to any others (a conclusion that does not follow because they can at least be contrasted, which is a kind of comparison), then certainly they have given a bridgehead to their more extreme cousins, hermeneutic epistemological relativists.

Spiro attacks this group with vigor. First, he says, cultures are not unique. They share features, basically those deriving from our species—specific background (and others, too, historically derived, we may add). This is true. He goes on to say that human social and psychological characteristics are also determined by extra-cultural variables. These he lists as "ecology, biology, subsistence economy, social structure, socialization and the like" (Spiro

1986:267). Here we see the weakness of not having a definition of culture. Most of us might have supposed that economy, social structure, and socialization were somehow included in culture, but Spiro seems suddenly to have switched to, or invoked, "British" categories here, in which a conventional separation was made between culture and social structure. But this only underscores the need to have a definition of what is left in culture when all these things are excluded from it.

He further suddenly introduces the idea of universal functional prerequisites as a means of preserving universals in the face of variability. Theories, however, must address themselves to that variability as well as to such hypothesized prerequisites. This relates to the rest of Spiro's argument, in which he discusses whether anthropology can be scientific.

Epistemological relativists (ER), he says, are concerned only with the meanings found in particular cultures which they attempt to interpret or translate. Again, much depends on the meaning of "interpret" here. It could mean "to make sense of by reference to an overall theory," in which case interpretive anthropology would also be explanatory if not scientific. Victor Turner's work is actually of this kind. But Spiro restricts the meaning to a limited act of translation for the culture under investigation. Given this sense of the term, he rightly points out that the position of ER scholars is untenable, because if cultures are infinitely variable and thought is culturally determined we can neither understand nor translate across cultures. But ER scholars claim to do just that. Has their position been characterized rightly? For example, do they say that there are no *related* cultures? If there are, at least within the circle of these, translation is possible.

The second prong of Spiro's attack on ER scholars is to say that insofar as they eschew explanation and choose a particular form of interpretation they are being unscientific and indeed irresponsible. As I have noted, I certainly agree that anthropology can be a science, and in the general sense in which Spiro means that term. However, I am unhappy about his attitude toward interpretive work in anthropology. If there is anywhere in his paper that he is unfair, it is here. The point is that he privileges scientifically gained knowledge absolutely above all other forms of knowledge, to the extent that these other forms are "not intellectually responsible" (Spiro 1986:275). To be fair to Professor Spiro himself, he directs his attacks only at the notion that among variant "readings" of a situation none can be picked out as especially valid—an idea that needs more discussion. However, is this overall privilege given to science correct?

I think it is incorrect, because we do not know by science alone how to respond to everything that there is in the world. Emotions are a part of our response to the world, as are poetry and the imagination in general. These matters form a vital part of human experience. It is tendentious to exclude consideration of them from the roster of interests anthropologists should be allowed to have and to argue that those very species-specific intercultural capacities Spiro himself invokes should not be turned to the service of our subject. In other words, I would not dismiss humanistic knowledge so readily and disparagingly as Spiro does, nor would I permit that everything good in it be thrown out with the rejection of epistemological relativism. Interpretation, too, may involve cross-cultural generalization and theorizing, and if there is a psychic unity of humankind there is a basis for this. To conclude this part: I agree with the main thrust of Spiro's argument, which is to show that anthropology can be a science. However, I note that "normative relativism" gets left aside in the course of his text. I think this is not unrelated to my second point, that Spiro unnecessarily denigrates all humanistic scholarship within anthropology under the guise of expelling ER from the fold. Anthropology, in my view, can and should be both scientific and humanistic, and it is incorrect to say that to practice it in a humanistic manner is necessarily irresponsible, or at best a lowly first step toward scientific explanation. To the contrary, I would see science and humanism as equal partners in the study of human similarities and differences.

My remarks here also indicate my attitude toward the emic/etic issue. I have noted the persistent thrust within anthropology either to deny that it is a science or to drag it wholesale into some particular scientific format—to convert it either into a humanity or a science. Yet why should we not accept it as both?

In passing, it is necessary to comment on psychoanalytic theory. Although Spiro does not say so, it is this which he deploys as science in anthropology. I, however, would do the reverse, and paradoxically might find myself defending psychoanalysis, but on grounds opposite to those of Spiro and ones which he would reject. If we look at the actual use made by anthropologists of Freudian concepts, notably by Obeyesekere, we find that Freudian ideas are interwoven seamlessly in their texts. They are taken for granted, built into the narrative on a level with itself rather than tested. Thus, they really do form a part of the ethnography, but the part they play is one I would call interpretive and humanistic rather than scientific. As a scientist, I therefore remain unconvinced; as a humanist, or one participating in a tradition of Freudian thought, I *might* be more sympathetic to the attempt. But I have no idea how by such literary devices we are supposed to *test* the intended universality of Freudian ideas.

The reason why the kind of thorough-going, or radically critical, eclecticism I am inclined to adopt is unlikely to achieve general agreement is one that I also recognize as inevitable: it gets rid of certain forms of conflictual debate and so reduces for some the fun of disagreement and for others the pleasure of pontificating. Anthropologists certainly tend to get not only the tribes they deserve, but also the theories; and as characters differ so do theories. Indeed, theories are not just good to think with but to fight with, and many a department can be split along the lines of innatists versus culturalists or biological versus cultural anthropologists. American anthropology departments are as prone to this form of rift as British ones in the 1970s were to struggles between neo-Marxists and rearguard crypto-structural-functionalists, precisely because the American tradition is broad and embraces all the branches of anthropology. Under such a cover there is endless room for fierce disagreement, so that anthropology as a whole becomes in practice a kind of politics. The chief protagonist on the "scientific" side nowadays is less psychoanalysis than sociobiology. Sociobiology may be treated either as a form of political ideology or as a scientific theory. It is more polite to treat it as the latter, because *all* theories have some ideological input and all can be made to produce a further ideological output. Sociobiology is in this regard no different from any other theoretical paradigm seeking its hegemony. Like psychoanalysis, it is certainly rooted in

Western industrial society, but its stimulus comes in the first place from insect and animal studies. It homes in suddenly on anthropology by virtue of the fact that it takes note of the significance of kinship relations in all human societies, something anthropologists thought was theirs until the sociobiologists rudely snatched it from them and vastly expanded its universalist impact against its relativist variability. Culture is stripped down to biology, and biology is determinant; variability is relatively insignificant or is explained by the workings of universal principles in local historical or ecological settings. Despite the protests of anthropologists such as Sahlins, sociobiology's knock-down approach as a blatantly universal and explanatory theory certainly provides a major challenge to conventional anthropology. My response to it, however, is that its attempts to account for variability have lacked sophistication, and that to make its proper entry sociobiology must create a new ethnography. The more thoughtful sociobiologists would possibly agree with me here. I illustrate my ideas now with reference to that centerpiece of sociobiological theory, kin selection.

If kin selection is at work in human populations, one might expect there to be a species-specific form of kinship structure to express this principle. In fact, however, anthropologists have made a speciality, ever since Morgan, of discovering and describing different forms of kinship structure in human societies. They have not gone very far in explaining why these different forms do exist, but the mere fact that they undoubtedly are there and are a prominent feature of social variation is enough to show that a simple account of the workings of kin selection will not do.

Further, the data from social anthropology have been used to argue against the idea of kin selection in a more fundamental way. Not only do kin groups vary, but the idea of kinship itself varies. There is, of course, a considerable unresolved controversy over this point, but it is at any rate the case that in some societies the notion of kinship is not to be confined to a narrow conception of genealogical relatedness. Cultural categories exist which either generalize out from such a conception or indeed run counter to it. (I refer here to ideas of "substance.") Hence, the notion of a one-to-one correspondence between social kinship and genetic relatedness can be shown quite easily to be false. Social anthropologists such as Sahlins (1976) tend both to start and finish with that point, but this is an error. There are several more matters to explore here.

First, as Michael Ruse has pointed out, kin selection (and maximization of inclusive fitness, supposedly happening as its result) has to be seen along with reciprocal altruism between non-kin, nongenetically related persons (1979:109ff). Regarding Sahlins's idea that this will result in social selection, Ruse insists that reciprocal altruism still contributes to inclusive fitness because an individual will lose more by opting out than by responding to others in accordance with it. The force of this point presumably depends on circumstances, and its truth is not self-evident; but it is not hard to see both that it is potentially true and that individuals can assess costs and benefits in any society where social relations are fairly egalitarian and open. For that reason, it might well fit the earliest human societies, but its effects must surely be heavily masked if not contradicted in hierarchical arenas predicated precisely on certain *denials* of reciprocity between individuals. Be that as it may, the point is made that kin selection is not the only mechanism which sociobiologists invoke to explain the development of social groups. It is true, however, that they tend to relate the effects of activity always to the idea of inclusive fitness.

However, even if we accept that inclusive fitness may be an underlying factor in the evolution of kinship systems, we are not thereby committed to arguing that all human kinship systems should be the same. There are three reasons (that I can think of) why this is so. The first is that no one denies that human social systems exist in an ecological context and that ecological factors partly condition or place limits on the development of social groups. In order to survive at all, and thus to get to square one on the inclusive fitness matrix, human beings have to secure a living. Their efforts to do so have influenced the forms of kinship structure they have invented and maintained. It is true, though, that these "efforts to survive" are always intimately bound up with the organization of reproduction as well as production, and this is presumably why a commentator from quite a different tradition, Janet Siskind (1978), chooses to see kinship as itself a product of gender and a division of labor between the sexes. The interplay between ecology and human forms of reproduction can thus account for at least some variation in kinship structures. And this corresponds to the second overall reason why systems differ. No one denies that cultural evolution has in various ways replaced biological evolution in the case of humans, and that cultural evolution has a certain autonomous aspect that need not be in harmony with what we could expect from genetic evolution. If this is accepted as a general position, it follows that we can look for no more than *some* degrees of correspondence between cultural forms and sociobiological postulates, insofar as these are predicated on genetic mechanisms. It is still of interest to look for such degrees of correspondence and to see whether cultural forms do in general develop in the ways that evolutionary biologists would expect; but we do not have to argue that they should fit exactly. The approach should therefore be a problem-oriented one.

The third reason for variability is one that is more popular with sociobiologists. It is that degrees of genetic relatedness between those classified as belonging to a set of kin categories may in fact vary. Here one enters a field characterized by the use of two concepts, parental certainty and parental investment. For mothers, parenthood is certain and investment, therefore, unproblematic. For fathers, however, this is not so. Male paternity is always uncertain, though paternity tests are now refined enough to allow very little doubt. Concealed ovulation that has evolved in human females accentuates the problem for the male, so sociobiologists argue. The basic assumption, which comes from the heart of the theory, is that men will invest heavily in children only if they know these children do contain some of their own genes. The argument is cross-cut by another theoretical motif relating to sexual selection: women are expected to be more selective of mates than men and this can lead to conflict. Women's propensity to select would favor a male's paternity certainty, but men's propensity not to select would threaten to counter this. Competition between males is thus followed by attempts to secure sole access. When this is linked with accumulation, we have the kernel of a polygamous, male-dominant structure.

From this interest in paternity certainty there has emerged another line of reasoning, which suggests that if paternity certainty falls below a certain level then one would expect instead to find a man investing more heavily in his sister's children than in his wife's, since on balance there will be a greater likelihood that he shares genes with the sister's children (provided he knows that she is at least of the same mother as himself). This will not be so for brother's children, even if again the brother is definitely by the same mother, since the brother's wife may bear children to other men. The argument is then expanded to the systems level, and applied to explain what is known as the avunculate in social anthropological studies—that is, the prominence of a close relationship between mother's brother and sister's son. Further, most of the sociobiological writers seem to equate "the avunculate" with matrilineal systems of group affiliation.

I am going to look at this problem in greater detail, as it exemplifies clearly the difficulties we have in relating sociological and biological data and also the difficulty of explaining group variability.

First, the avunculate covers two different cases, the patrilineal and the matrilineal. Properly, it is applied only to the former, so the sociobiologists have in a sense caught hold of the wrong term for what they wish to explain. This is not, however, a fundamental stumbling block. In either case we can look to see if the predictions of theory are fulfilled.

In the patrilineal case, first examined by Radcliffe-Brown, a stern relationship with the father is counterbalanced by an affectionate or supportive one with the mother's brother. Radcliffe-Brown saw this as an extension of a warm relationship with the mother herself, although he also correlated it with bridewealth practices. Lévi-Strauss set it into a wider matrix of sibling and affinal, as well as parental and uncle/nephew ties. In Radcliffe-Brown's analysis, as refined by later writers such as Meyer Fortes and Jack Goody, the explanatory element becomes the jural structure of the society itself. Jural ties with the father and his lineage are balanced, through cultural prescription, against moral and affective ties with mother and her lineage. Goody in particular showed that "MB" may refer to several different persons and is generalized as a category to include whole sets of people. Further, it is characterized by reciprocal duties on the part of the sister's children toward these categories of uncle. Seen in this light, the expanded mother's brother/sister's son (MB/ZS) relationship simply does not yield to the sociobiological perspective. It is too complicated socially and culturally to be subsumed under a notion of quasi-parental "investment." This is also true of Melanesian cases, where one can show that often the MB is indeed seen as an "owner" of the child and has supernatural powers in relation to the Z child: for example, he may be able to curse the child and make it sick or prevent it from growing. In Pangia, one of the field areas in which I have done research, the MB's authoritative powers are very marked; payments of wealth to "redeem" one's "skin" and ensure health must continually be made by the Z child's father and later by himself. And MB for example may spit on the Z child's skin and cause a permanent attack of warts that cannot be removed unless the MB is placated by gifts. This emphasis on the possible hostile powers of the MB does not look like "parental investment" either, although it is true that the MB does also take a close interest in the Z child's welfare.

In the matrilineal case the argument for the sociobiological viewpoint is stronger. The logical operator, it will be recalled, is paternity certainty. If this is lowered, men will invest more in their sisters' children. Matrilineal systems are held either to conduce to this state of affairs or to issue from it, or both. Jeffrey Kurland has written the most elaborate discussion of this view, following earlier work by Richard Alexander (Kurland 1979, and References). The mechanism whereby paternity certainty is lowered is presented as sexual promiscuity or "philandering," as Alexander sometimes puts it with quaint ethnocentrism. So it is suggested that, in general, matrilineal systems show a greater tendency toward such promiscuity, and the famous cases of the Nayar and the Trobriands are cited in support of this view. The evidence is suggestive and in line with what social anthropologists have observed frequently in matrilineal systems: there is no *simple* response to the rules; the rules themselves generate a number of solutions by way of residence and affiliation, and in particular high-status men tend to claim both Z children and their own. This is true both of the Trobriands and the Central African cases—Bemba, Mayombe, and others—first studied by Audrey Richards. Kurland, it should be noted, explicitly eschews a "causal" argument so that he is not arguing that matriliny emerges because of paternity uncertainty. He writes:

> These aspects of human sociality and biology do seem to correlate, but clearly this association must be mediated by a host of biological, demographic, economic, and psychological variables that are at present rather imperfectly understood. Simplicity and comprehensibility, virtues of the scientific model, are also sometimes its major weakness when realism is lacking. (1979:175–176)

What does seem lacking here, then, is any coherent argument that a system as such is likely to emerge for reasons stemming from the sociobiological premise. If not, then the most we can be looking for, again, is the correspondence approach, or a systems approach in which we would argue that a factor such as paternity uncertainty is likely to increase over time, thus conducing towards a greater stress on matrilineal ties.

Kurland does have very interesting things to say about the Trobriand case, which can be cited as raising an acute difficulty for his basic argument. This point also takes us back to one I initially touched on, the definition of kinship. The Trobriand theory of kinship specifically denies paternity in the sense understood in Western folk theories of conception. Yet an important social role is accorded to the mother's husband, and elaborate exchanges tie affines together. Moreover, husbands are jealous of their wives' adultery, and wives of their husbands'. Kurland interprets the denial of paternity in two ways: one, a strategy by matrilineal kin to keep resources for investment within the matriline. In view of recent analyses of Trobriands kinship, this is probably oversimplified, but it has some truth. Second, Kurland suggests that "paternity ignorance represents a rather impressive 'smoke screen' for increased promiscuity"—with the covert aim of actually also increasing one's reproductive success (1979:174). Only the Trobriand ethnographers could settle that one, if they have data bearing on it. It will be noted that Kurland is assuming that there is an underlying "natural" set of strategies beneath the Trobriand cultural code. He assumes, for example, that males covertly do wish to have information about paternity and do make a link between intercourse and conception. This is a very a difficult matter. The precise Trobriand dogma is that males "mould" (*kopo'i*) their children's external appearance, though the child is in fact a *baloma*, a spirit reincarnated from the mother's sub-clan, or *dala*. Can these ideas be equated with notions such as "paternity certainty"? In some ways, clearly, they cannot; and if sociobiology depended on them doing so its case would be weakened. But, when faced with difficulties of this sort, some sociobiologists tend to argue that people don't have to be consciously aware of their strategies at all, since in any case they have been "selected" to behave in the way they do. The trouble with this argument is that it suggests what is so far not shown, that the behavioral strategies we are examining are genetically and *not* culturally programmed. A more acceptable approach, as I have argued, is to see whether the cultural ideas can or cannot themselves be interpreted as reflecting sociobiological principles *without* assuming that if so the system is under genetic control as such. This would help to meet the problem that cultural and genetic evolution proceed at different rates, culture allowing for much swifter change. Strategies, with underlying biological aims, may be invented at the cultural level much faster than people can be "selected" to do things unconsciously.

This matter of consciousness brings me to a further question: the mechanisms whereby close kin are "recognized." Sociobiologists agree that people need not be able to calculate fractions (or to do algebra) in order to recognize close kin. How, then, do they do it? The standard answer is astoundingly simple: people have a propensity to cooperate with and help those they have been brought up with, and if these happen to be close kin then they also act to maximize inclusive fitness. This answer is also damaging to the idea that we are actually maximizing inclusive fitness all the time, since it suggests that the basic thing which was evolved is the mechanism itself and that in principle we can cooperate with anyone who is brought up along with us. I find it difficult to see how this is not also potentially very damaging to the basic idea of kin selection. It reads like an admission that Sahlins is right after all and we have group variability because we are able to cooperate with people regardless of any strict tie of genealogical kinship.

Here again, however, the matter cannot rest. This variability is not so variable. It is a matter of note that in all human societies some importance is accorded to genealogical kinship and that in most there are ways of calculating ego's closeness of relationship to others in addition to broad sociocentric classifications in which kinship is metaphorized into group identity. The formation of groups can also be seen as a kind of coalition-making for defense or aid in obtaining spouses and allies—in other words, it can be interpreted in terms of inclusive fitness, reciprocal altruism, and sexual selection, as Chagnon does for the Yanomamo (Chagnon 1979). In modern industrialized societies, the persistence of the nuclear family, as well as processes attendant on its weakening (e.g., conflict over custody of children), creates problems for analysis which are at least amenable to sociobiological hypotheses. To use them we would have to recognize that, for reasons which lie outside of the provenance of sociobiology, kinship in these societies does not have the obvious "extended" categories it has in tribal society, and "investment" is much narrowed down as well as influenced by class attitudes. If so, then the remaining core of relationships must be particularly vital to study. If inclusive fitness is narrowed down so as almost to be equated with reproductive success, and if this success is of the K rather than the r type, then one would expect to see very heavy investment in small numbers of children and very clear limitation of numbers of children.

Let me now try to summarize what I think are the chief points emerging from this sketchy review:

1. Sociobiologists must make up their minds whether they seek to explain the origins and transformations of cultural systems or whether they aim simply to uncover biological correlates and implications of these systems as they exist today.
2. As a research strategy, sociobiologists have to concentrate on behavioral patterns, what people actually do. They will then

be faced with the standard problems of the relationship between behavior and ideology which turn up in ethnographic
fieldwork.

3. Another point—the relationship between cultural and biological selection—has to be made clear before biological and social
anthropologists can effectively communicate.

4. On the particular problems of parental investment and inclusive
fitness, it is clear that social anthropologists could help by
(a) showing how complex it would be to measure "investment"
and reduce a multiplicity of features of relationships to this
yardstick, and (b) indicating how people themselves see closeness or distance of kin and how their perceptions can be interpreted as parts of overall strategies, either of themselves as
individuals, or of groups acting in an ecological and political
context. In other words, even sociobiology cannot in the end
stay clear of the emic context, because the peoples' own categories need to be understood if only as a means of comparing
them with those of the sociobiologist.

A more general point can also be raised here: How *much*
would we expect sociobiology to explain? It is the same question
I ask of every theory, and my aim is the same: to keep theories
in their place so that they do not become too imperialistic.
Such an aim is, of course, diametrically opposite that of those
who believe one theory can and must explain everything. I,
on the contrary, think that theories can explain only what they
are designed to explain, and this tends to be a specific aspect
of things, not everything. I even am happy to reserve an
area for things not explained or perhaps not explicable: for
curiosity, for puzzlement, for mystery, and for fun. I suppose this
makes me at least a humanist, though I also practice science. In
any case, I feel that Sperber's aphorism can be extended further:
all keys to human behavior are themselves a part of such behavior. In that sense, they are all arguably emic after all, and
with this kick across the pitch of systemics we could suggest
that emics win over etics, in the extra time suddenly granted by
this last insight.

References

Chagnon, Napoleon A.
  1979   Male Competition Favoring Close Kin, and Village Fissioning among the Yanomamo Indians. In *Evolutionary Biology and Human Social Behaviors*, edited by Napoleon A. Chagnon and William Irons, pp. 86–131. Duxbury Press, North Scituate, Mass.

Fortes, Meyer
  1987   *Religion, Morality and the Person: Essays on Tallensi Religion*. Edited by Jack Goody. Cambridge University Press, Cambridge.

Horton, Robin
  1983   Social Psychologies: African and Western. In *Oedipus and Job in West African Religion*, edited by Meyer Fortes and Robin Horton, pp. 41–82. Cambridge University Press, Cambridge.

Horton, Robin, and Ruth Finnegan (editors)
  1973   *Modes of Thought*. Faber and Faber, London.

Kurland, Jeffrey A.
  1979   Paternity, Mother's Brother, and Human Sociality. In *Evolutionary Biology and Human Social Behavior: An Anthropological Perspective*, edited by Napoleon A. Chagnon and William G. Irons, pp. 145–180. Duxbury Press, North Scituate, Mass.

Leach, Edmund
  1954   *Political Systems of Highland Burma*. G. Bell and Sons, London.

Lutz, Catherine
  1985   Ethnopsychology Compared to What? Explaining Behavior and Consequences among the Ifaluk. In *Person, Self and Experience*, edited by Geoffrey White and John Kirkpatrick, pp. 35–79. University of California Press, Berkeley.
  1988   *Unnatural Emotions: Everyday Sentiments on a Micronesian Atoll and Their Challenge to Western Theory*. University of Chicago Press, Chicago.

Marcus, George, and Michael Fischer
  1986   *Anthropology as Cultural Critique: An Experimental Moment in the Human Sciences*. University of Chicago Press, Chicago.

Meeker, Michael E.
  1979   *Literature and Violence in North Arabia*. Cambridge University Press, Cambridge.

Obeyesekere, Gananath
  1981   *Medusa's Hair: An Essay on Personal Symbols and Religious Experience*. University of Chicago Press, Chicago.

Ruse, Michael

1979   *Sociobiology, Sense or Nonsense?* D. Reidel, Boston.

Sahlins, Marshall D.

1976   *Culture and Practical Reason.* University of Chicago Press, Chicago.

Siskind, Janet

1978   *To Hunt in the Morning.* Oxford University Press, New York.

Sperber, Dan

1975   *Rethinking Symbolism.* Translated by Alice Morton. Cambridge University Press, Cambridge.

1985   *On Anthropological Knowledge.* Cambridge University Press, Cambridge.

Spiro, Melford

1986   Cultural Relativism and the Future of Anthropology. *Cultural Anthropology* 1(3):259–286.

Strathern, Andrew J.

1971   *The Rope of Moka.* Cambridge University Press, Cambridge.

1984   *A Line of Power.* Tavistock, London.

Taussig, Michael

1987   *Shamanism, Colonialism and the Wild Man.* University of Chicago Press, Chicago.

Turner, Victor

1969   *The Ritual Process: Structure and Anti-Structure.* Aldine, Chicago.

Anthropology's Odyssey

1989

To some of its practitioners, anthropology either is, or must be converted into, a severe science, dependent above all on hypotheses and quantitative methods for testing these. To others it is a philosophical subject enabling us to reflect in a very general way on both universal and varying patterns of behavior. To yet others it is a subject of the imagination, demanding insight, creativity, and an expressive style of communication. For me it is certainly all three of these, and much more. I conceptualize anthropology as a journey—wide-ranging, hazardous, exotic—with a desire, perhaps not to be fulfilled, to reach home, so that in understanding others we at the same time understand ourselves—giving identity and also receiving it in the same intellectual quest. This quest has led me from place to place around the world, and most recently to Pittsburgh. Throughout the years I have primarily identified myself as a fieldworker and ethnographer interested in the part of the world known as Melanesia. This remains true. While giving some account of my work in the Melanesian island of New Guinea, I also want to stand back a little and review some trends in anthropology as a whole, particularly as these strike those who, like myself, have moved between a number of traditions and concerns in the subject, as these vary in different countries where anthropology is practiced. Anthropology is certainly a science, but not *only* that; and although science is international, countries maintain their own particular brands of it, while also developing stereotypes of varying cogency about other traditions.

The material for this chapter is from my inaugural lecture as Andrew W. Mellon Professor of Anthropology at the University of Pittsburgh given on January 24, 1989.

A metaphor of a bridge appeals to me when I consider how to say what anthropology is. Anthropology is a bridge between ourselves and others, whether these others be distant in space or time. Putting it this way also tells us a little more than just stating that anthropologists study people, scientifically or otherwise. It implies that serious gaps exist and that the bridges have to be constructed carefully or else they will break. It implies, too, that we want to cross over. And finally it suggests that if we make such a bridge, then in certain cases the movement across it can be reciprocal.

These two metaphors, that of the journey and the bridge, in effect join together and become a single idea: that anthropology is a movement, a lively play of the mind that enables us to pass—by solid trekking and at times by leaps—into terrains of experience and knowledge which otherwise would be denied to us. Whether our approach is idiographic or nomothetic, to conceptualize ourselves as travelers and searchers is surely an idea that enables us to keep looking ahead rather than merely backwards; indeed, to strain our eyes to the horizon and look to the future.

Such a perspective is all the more important for anthropology, I think, because it has been a favorite habit of other writers in related fields such as politics, history, literature, or sociology to announce the imminent death of our subject or even to invite others to its funeral without checking whether the patient is in fact dead or just temporarily dazed by the kind of soul-loss feeling that comes from seeing another snatch your ideas, declare them his own, then denounce you for not having had them—a mind-blowing act, but one which I assure you is not unknown in academia and is closely comparable to certain kinds of sorcery or witchcraft practiced on victims in Melanesian cultures! Yet, however much it is apparently sorcerized or even cannibalized, anthropology survives and always will do so, precisely because it brings to its subject matter a viewpoint that is holistic, various, imaginative, and unbounded by time and place.

The first hurdle, then, that anthropologists have to overcome is the idea that their subject matter is dying. There is no doubt that, for particular reasons in the nineteenth century, anthropology began as the study of "the primitive." One such reason was the search for origins stimulated by Darwin's theory of the origins of species and another was the drive of Victorian thinkers to represent their form of society as at the apex of the tree of civilization—a peculiar combination of scientific and ideological concerns out of which anthropology was first born but which it has since outgrown. The Victorians, of course, equated contemporary tribal societies with early societies in general, and none more so than those of aboriginal Australia and New Guinea; this is a viewpoint which persists unmodified in popular discourse to this day. Although I have for years studied precisely the societies once labeled in that way, I have no hesitation in rejecting any view that anthropology is somehow intrinsically limited to the investigation of "the primitive." What we have carried over from such studies into other contexts is, first, a sensitivity toward the interplay of sameness and difference that strikes us whenever we encounter a relatively unknown culture; second, a realization that to apprehend this interplay we need special methods of study; and third, a bundle of theories about social and cultural processes that can be extrapolated exponentially from case to case.

All these tools in our kit are means whereby we initially approach an unknown culture. But they can be turned to good use in studying our own, or related, cultures also, simply because they start from the premise that we cannot prejudge the context we are looking at, that the surprising may lurk in the familiar, or that we actually do not know our own milieu so well after all. There is the particular benefit to be gained when a stranger turns the eye of the other upon us; but we can also, through anthropology, do the same, at least partly, for ourselves.

Why did anyone think that the subject matter of anthropology was dying? Because, as I have already implied, this was defined as a certain kind of aboriginal, tribal society, and because such societies had all been, to a greater or lesser degree, aggressively influenced by the outside world. Marxist anthropologists at one point even attempted to deliver a final body blow to anthropology by arguing that tribal societies were in fact not aboriginal at all but had been much more influenced by outside forces than was earlier allowed. These perspectives carried some force, but they were exaggerated. First, even though tribal societies have indeed been influenced by changes, this does not mean they turn into replicas of metropolitan countries overnight, or even in the long run. Second, even though such influences began long ago, the same point holds: each new case has something to tell us about processes of change, degrees of cultural freedom and constraint, and historical variation. In other words, to show that people have been influenced by the capitalist world does not mean that their social order has *ipso facto* been produced by capitalism. As always, the true spirit of Marx's sense of inquiry, rather than a mechanical Marx-*ism* is what is needed here: that is, an appreciation of the fundamental dialectics of relationships, not in terms of unilateral causation but of reciprocal influence and reformulation.

So much for a preamble. I have claimed anthropology as a movement—a movement back and forth between cultures, across swaying bridges that we attempt to strengthen by hypotheses, data collection, and theories. The success of this movement depends both on there actually being processes common to all the cultures we look at and on our conceptualization of these by means of theory building. It is now up to me to illustrate all these asseverations with some cases.

Some anthropologists look for a basis of commonality in psychological theory, for instance in Freudian ideas; others search for it in biology by looking at aggression in ethological terms as a genetically derived response, for example, or by arguing that the maximization of reproductive fitness is the underlying drive in humans. Others, again, look for universal political processes. Which approach one chooses seems to me to be a matter of taste or inclination rather than of scientificity itself. Although I am interested in all approaches, I myself tend toward the view that political processes are fundamental and can be observed cross-culturally, operating in much the same way in a faculty meeting as in a New Guinea ceremonial house—give or take some important cultural factors. But cultural factors also influence politics, and do so in ways that are not always apparent even to the social actors themselves. Any case, therefore, must be looked at from both angles, the local and the comparative.

Today, therefore, we are far from an earlier view that implicitly prevailed, to effect that anthropology is intrinsically and ineradicably concerned only with a certain range of societies, those labeled as "primitive"; and that when we switch to discussion of Western society or of tribal societies undergoing change, we turn overnight into sociologists. No matter what we call ourselves, however, what counts is the essential consistency or continuity of approach we bring to a problem, and this is achieved by the definition of the overall problem itself. In any case, the practices of anthropologists have long out-run any artificial concern with the "primitive" world. One well-known anthropologist who has made the transition in his writings between "the other" and "ourselves" is Freddie Bailey, a British social anthropologist who began his career with fieldwork in a remote part of rural India, Orissa; continued it by directing a series of studies of local communities in Europe; and finally turned his pen inward on the academic world itself, examining the politics of interaction at committee and departmental meetings. Bailey's approach has throughout been rather "hard-nosed." He constructs individuals and groups as essentially self-seeking and concerned with their relative status and power vis-à-vis one another, and society as the arena in which contests for these values are enacted and more or less controlled. The way in which this happens in an Indian village is, of course, ethnographically different from the way it happens on a university campus; but the "it" involved is portrayed as essentially the same, and by this we see that what unifies the approach is a certain view of human political behavior. Bailey is skeptical about altruism or ideals and is receptive to notions of selfishness and pragmatism. Of course, people may employ altruistic-sounding arguments in order to support their own interests, but this does not alter their fundamental aims, which the investigator has to uncover. Bailey began his work on this theme of academic life by arguing that at meetings academics adopt a certain set of roles, which he called "masks," and that they select these according to their needs at the time. Bailey's categories of masks are intended to fit cross-culturally, and no doubt they do, but there is one possibility that he has not so far explored systematically, and this is the difference between British and American academic life. Bailey moved in mid-career from Sussex to San Diego, from the chilly waves of Brighton to the warm roller coasters of California. One might have expected him to encounter another "sea change" in political behavior, and in one crucial respect he almost certainly did. In Britain, "the Professor" is usually also a permanently appointed head of department and in theory, therefore, has much more power than the American counterpart, the departmental chair, who is elected to this position for varying periods of time. The difference this structural change makes to the running of departments in general and meetings in particular would be well worth attention, and it is one that has been forced on me since my arrival in Pittsburgh. Is the American system more democratic or more egalitarian than the British one? Making everyone into a "Professor" might seem to be a move in this direction, but reality is naturally more complicated than this. Many bid for power, and there are various avenues for achieving it; but not so many succeed after all. There are competing and cross-cutting factions; there is ambiguity and maneuvering; there are implicit ideologies and agendas. In short, there are all the elements which political anthropologists are accustomed to look for in rural villages in northern India or the New Guinea Highlands—with the only difference being that the ethnographic materials are immediately on our doorsteps rather than 10,000 miles away. Since the 1960s, we have seen an efflorescence of studies entitled "The anthropology of X," but the anthropology of departments of anthropology remains a relatively undeveloped field of study. I have been led to this problem less for theoretical than for practical reasons, since in my own minor odyssey from place to place I have participated in the lives of such departments in Cambridge, Canberra, Port Moresby, London, and, finally, Pittsburgh. The most obvious difference between the English and the American departments I have already pointed out; another is one for which I gained some preparation in both Cambridge and London, and that is the divided unity or united division of departments into physical and cultural anthropology, archaeology, and linguistics. Apart from being a historical residue of an older European system introduced by Franz Boas, this situation gives the possibility of making worthwhile connections across the spectrum of the subject as a whole while carrying with it in practice the enhanced likelihood of factionalism in which each segment attempts to achieve a hegemony or prominence either by emphasizing its distinctiveness or, conversely, by attempting to re-define the whole subject in terms of its own image: a micropolitical use of metaphor and metonymy by means of which overall evaluations of the work of others are attempted. This process is carried forward into the graduate level in a way that is quite different from the British system. In London at University College, for example, undergraduate students certainly studied all branches of the subject for their first degree; but at graduate level this ceased and they invariably specialized in one part of the discipline. This made the process of graduate training more straightforward and less time-consuming than it is here. I must confess that when I came to America and realized the labyrinthine complexity of courses, classes, grades, requirements, and options that enclose the life of the graduate student, I then realized that the term "school," which at first I thought was an amusement, was something that operates in all seriousness. Of course, this difference is based on further differences in the educational system, in particular on the relative lack of really specialized undergraduate degrees in the arts here, which means that the foundation for early differentiation at graduate level is lacking. But this does not justify imposing a totally set format on all graduate students regardless of their backgrounds and countries of origin. The American "melting pot" should not be allowed to transmogrify itself into an intellectual straitjacket. Nor should the purpose of graduate school be to memorize huge numbers of facts; rather, it should be to define and investigate problems.

All this, however, is intended not so much as a criticism as by way of a digression or a prelude to my more substantive themes. I work in a rather traditionally defined sector of sociocultural anthropology, and I see that a problem for those in this sector nowadays is the old one of self-definition. Sociocultural anthropology potentially takes the whole world as its ethnographic province, yet it has no single unified theory comparable to the physical sciences' theory of evolution to guide it. As a result, it splits into area-based, theory-based, methodology-based, topic-based, etc., particularities, and each department emerges with a collocation of these instances, which have then to be welded into some form of coherence or else must be allowed to flourish randomly. The problem is compounded by the fact that in present-day America there is a blending of the British and American traditions—the British being much more cohesive and limited, and the American more loose and expansive. It is no small wonder that for an apparently growing number of practitioners there has been a retreat into a melange of texts, and clever remarks about them, so that cultural anthropology becomes a potpourri of literature, history, and philosophy clearly announcing its open-ended lack of theory while claiming for itself at least an amusing style. However, we can write well while still keeping our quest for theory steadily in view. There is a great opportunity to do this nowadays, but not through the metonymic or synecdochal political processes to which I have earlier alluded. Sociocultural anthropology cannot find its identity by being either turned into literary criticism or by being biologized or even psychologized, although there is a stronger tradition of this last tendency here in America than in the United Kingdom. Rather, the kind of overall approach that needs to be taken is much more pragmatic. Given each of our skills and specialties how can we relate these to broader issues? I will show some answers to this question in three different ways: first, in relation to some recent work of mine in my geographical field of study, Melanesia; second, in relation to a topical or subdisciplinary field I would like to see developed here, medical anthropology; and finally, in relation to overall theory, where I shall take my cue from a recent book by Robert Hinde on links between ethology and the social sciences.

Guns and Revenge: The Body of the State

Revenge as a motive for hostile acts is frequently found to be a mechanism triggering violent escalations of conflict, whether this be in New Guinea or in major theaters of hostility between large countries of the metropolitan world. I have been studying the political affairs of one small group of people, the Kawelka tribe of Mount Hagen in the Western Highlands Province of Papua New Guinea since 1964. In 1964, this tribe, like others in its area, lived at peace with its neighbors under Australian colonial rule, effectively begun after 1945 and greatly facilitated by the Australians' possession of valuable shells that the local people used in their own exchanges. Access to these shells had in pre-colonial times been much more limited. The colonial regime thus depended for its initial success with the local people both on the import of shells into the region and on the occasional show of force by means of guns. The shell economy broke, however, under the sustained impact of over-supply, and shells were then discarded in favor of money, which the people incorporated into their exchanges as well as using it for purchases and payments within the new capitalist economy. In a continuous interweaving of neotraditional and introduced activities they attempted constantly to refashion their lives while still retaining past forms that continued to be important to them. The key to much of this retention of custom is political: as long as the society remains divided into clans and tribes with separate historical identities, cleavages, and alliances, there remains an enduring niche for the ceremonial means by which these relations are marked. Political structures have been much widened and overlaid by the introduction of local government councils, provincial-level government with elected representatives, and a national parliament, also with a separate range of MPs. But all of these introduced structures are influenced by the primordial political groupings, and tribal politics become closely intertwined with elections and power struggles in the introduced arena. Finally, men who have become important in business activities, and thus are looked upon as a new version of the "big-man" type of leader in exchanges, are invariably involved in politics as well, either standing for election themselves or else acting as prominent supporters and financiers for others.

Throughout the 1970s it was evident that peaceful intercourse between groups depended as much on this maintenance of the neotraditional nexus of activities as on the formal institutions of the state. The latter can be seen as supplying only the negative sanction of force, whereas the former give positive incentives and meanings. But this neotraditional nexus also carries its negative side. Most of the exchanges which are made are redressive, correcting incidents of violent killings from the past, but the negative cycle of these killings can at any time be regenerated by further hostilities. Alcohol consumption, road accidents, and urban brawls as well as renewed disputes over land use all contribute to this side of the cycle, and these are also patterns which increase with the growth of economic development through cash cropping in coffee and vegetables. In Hagen, as in so many New Guinea societies, it is an obligation either to exact revenge for a killing or to demand a large compensation gift. This traditional motivation remains firmly ingrained in people's ideas: political pride and necessity go hand-in-hand in maintaining it. It can even happen that a compensation payment is offered and accepted, yet still at some level hatred and suspicion continue and issue later in a further bout of killings. The cycle of exchanges stands in opposition to the cycle of killings, and a precarious balance is held between them over time. However, this balance has most recently been threatened by a step-up in technology, the introduction of guns into warfare. Initially, the colonial government retained a monopoly of these weapons, then a limited number were permitted for use, under license from the police, by local people as well as expatriates. For the people, guns were prestige items, used for hunting purposes. In no case were they deployed as weapons to kill human beings at this time. This is in itself a remarkable fact. Throughout the 1970s fighting, when it took place, was carried out entirely with bows, arrows, and spears. This separation of guns from warfare is to be explained largely by the fact that the owners of shotguns were older men, community leaders who gained their prestige more from exchanges than from disputes and open violence. This separation was also because of the limited supply of guns. These two circumstances were breached in 1985 by a new development in the society, the emergence of gangs of young men who stole cars and money, committed rape, broke into houses, and shot people. At first these gangs were confined to coastal towns of Papua New Guinea, but they soon had Highlands members, who eventually brought the practice back to the rural areas of the Highlands. With gangs came guns, and in greater and less controlled supply than ever before. Not only did gangs illegally gain possession of guns through hold-ups on the coast, they also, most significantly, began to build their own rudimentary versions of these weapons from pieces of piping and carved wooden stocks, and firing mechanisms were based on the release of a pin held in tension by a spring. The resulting artifacts were not exactly reliable, but they could be mass-manufactured and could thus become potentially feasible substitutes for the traditional bows, arrows, and spears. At the same time, a few really high-powered guns entered the area, either via the criminal gangs or indigenous businessmen with overseas contacts, or else through the police and army themselves. The combination of circumstances proved too much for the precariously preserved arena of tribal fighting. Guns entered this arena and rapidly became dominant in it, repeating patterns of swift change experienced at least three times before in the course of history: when the sweet potato replaced taro as a staple crop in prehistoric times; when the steel axe replaced stone tools early on in colonial history; and when money replaced shells in the 1970s. Crops, tools, media of exchange, and now weapons have successively been the focus of sudden change.

Standing back from the details of this history and asking general questions about its significance, we can see it as an example of the tribal response over time to introduced change. There is a period of latency. A new kind of technology becomes available, but this does not immediately change the society at large because it is confined to a particular, small role in which its full potentials are not realized. Its wider adoption into the political system is both inhibited negatively by the presence of the state and is delayed by the lack of supply. The social emergence of a new class then becomes the historical trigger of the situation, both literally and metaphorically. Meanwhile, ideology remains mostly unchanged, waiting to engage powerfully with whatever other historical elements emerge. Guns both enable this ideology to be played out more dramatically than ever before and also point towards a possible dissolution of the strict conditions of its reproduction. In the past killings and compensation were held in balance. With a huge increase in the ability to kill, it is difficult to see how this balance can be kept. Herein lies the major political problem for these people in the future. While anthropology enables us to analyze or identify this problem clearly, it does not enable us to predict what historical answer will be made to it. Yet whatever the solution is, it will have to be in the broader sense one which is constrained by "the economy of politics": the reconstruction of an equilibrium, however partial, between negative and positive political acts—in other words, the same basic process which takes place between nation states.

The State of the Body

The British social anthropologist Mary Douglas pointed out in two seminal works, *Purity and Danger* (1966) and *Natural Symbols* (1970), that the human body often becomes a vehicle for symbolic statements about cultural values or political power relationships. If political anthropology is conceived of, in part, as a study of the body of the state, medical anthropology is its metaphorical inverse, the study of the state of the body. Medical anthropology has been growing rapidly in America over the last decade. It is one of those diversifying subfields in the discipline as a whole which answers to certain trends of the time. What is important is to ensure that its theory and methods are still related to wider traditions and principles of investigation in anthropology as a whole and are not swamped by a flood of concerns that would draw its practitioners further and further away from anthropology as such. The theoretical propositions of Mary Douglas provide one of the frameworks needed to encompass this goal. Related to this is the approach via ethnomedicine, the study of cross-culturally variant categories and classifications having to do with health or illness and its treatment. Another foundation for medical anthropology has been elaborated by Horacio Fabrega of the Western Pennsylvania Psychiatric Institute in Pittsburgh, who distinguishes between "disease" and "illness" (Fabrega 1974). Whereas "disease" relates to an identifiable condition, as conceptualized in Western biomedicine, "illness" relates to the wider sociocultural context into which any such condition is set and expresses also the social role behavior of the sick person as well as the cultural values that are pursued through the *fact* of illness, for example prescribed ideals concerning response to pain and threat of the loss of life. Following this original insight, Margaret Lock and Nancy Scheper-Hughes have provided a reconceptualization of the body called "The Mindful Body." They distinguish between three bodies, the individual, the social, and the political. The individual body is the body-self as experienced by individuals cross-culturally, although ideas even at this level are culturally distinct. To this level corresponds also the disease concept as developed in biomedicine. The social body as the authors define it, refers to "the representational uses of the body as a natural symbol"—that is, the Mary Douglas level. The political body, or body politic, refers to "the regulation, surveillance, and control of bodies . . . in reproduction and sexuality, in work and in leisure, in sickness and other forms of deviance and human difference" (Lock and Scheper-Hughes 1987:7–8). This third level is the most wide-ranging, with the greatest implications for sociological and political analysis. What has to be remembered is that through all the levels we continue to be speaking about the biological body as an ultimate material referent, but at the social and political levels we are also speaking about the whole person. For medical anthropology a special interest lies in the interrelations between the levels, especially on how facts at the individual level feed into the other two, and vice-versa.

Lock and Scheper-Hughes in this article are also concerned, as many others have been, with reminding Western readers of the Cartesian specificity of ideas of mind and body that are a part of the biomedical tradition. In tribal societies what we separate as mind and body are regarded as tightly related, and therapy is directed at the whole person. In practice this means that whereas in biomedicine there is overemphasis on the body, in tribal medicine it looks to us as though there is an overemphasis on the mind. In fact, however, it is the "person" that is being treated as a whole entity. Biomedicine achieved great advances by taking a strictly materialist view which ignored "mind." Psychiatry and psychosomatic medicine had then to be reinvented in order to put back the other part of the equation that had dropped out. Most recently, advances in neurobiology tend to show that there are material links between chemical states of the brain and social conditions. In some instances, this may show that there is a genetic or at least a biological basis for conditions which have been thought to be caused by social circumstances reacting on the psychology of the individual; for example, schizophrenia. But reductionist explanations of this kind simply confine themselves to a reduced sphere of discourse. For medical anthropology the social and political levels remain always important, as they must also for diagnosticians interested in epidemiological patterns. Epidemiology itself has passed from a stage of rather straightforward collection of statistics on fertility, morbidity, and mortality to a more sophisticated appreciation of the "webs of causation" that are involved in historical changes of the incidence of disease. These webs always involve social factors outside of the individual, and the more epidemiology engages itself with these the more it metamorphoses itself into medical anthropology.

Another point that emerges out of the work of Lock and Scheper-Hughes, and which is implied in their title "The Mindful Body," is that the category of "psychosomatic" illness has to be rethought. At the moment, it occupies a midpoint between psychiatric illness, which supposedly has to do only with "mind," and biomedically defined conditions which are of the "body." The midpoint between these becomes, in this classification, a set of anomalies; yet in fact many biomedical conditions, such as heart attacks, clearly have their roots at least partly in the mental sphere, and this in turn is obviously influenced by the social conditions affecting diet, stress, and exercise of the individual. A further controversy centers around the concept of "Type A personalities," as they are called, whose own harshness may lead to heart attacks more often than occurs with the so-called "Type B," who are quieter and less competitively aggressive. A later phase of the original research shows that whereas Type A men surveyed were more liable to suffer an attack, they were also more likely to recover from it than Type B males. The same quality of drive that put them initially at risk also gave them an advantage in the context of actual illness. My point here would be that it may also be a mistake to "psychologize" the data by inventing the category Type A in the first place. Isolating a number of *only possibly* interrelated characteristics and then labeling them as a "type" may be no more valid in psychology than it was correct in anthropology to invent labels for whole cultures, such as the American anthropologist Ruth Benedict did in calling cultures Dionysian or Apollonian. The danger is that the hypostasized type, instead of being an explanandum, moves into the status of an explanans. Rather, we should emphasize the sociogenic circumstances involved. In the broadest sense, it is the society which "causes" these events through a multiplicity of influences, although we still have to deal with the fact that individuals react differently to the same conditions. This is a well-known kind of problem in the social sciences, and it has challenged us at least since Durkheim's statistical study of the incidence of suicide in different European countries. But, however we look on the arguments about Type A and Type B personalities, it is generally obvious that the mental does affect the physical just as much as the physical does the mental, and that the category of "psychosomatic," so far from being anomalous, has to be made central for medical anthropologists, if not for medical practitioners.

I find it interesting, and instructive, to realize that this insight is one that, in a sense, I learned from the peoples with whom I have worked for so long in Papua New Guinea. Like many tribal peoples, they conceive an individual's emotions as having a powerful influence over the physical state. In particular, they say that "anger" causes sickness. The term I gloss as "anger" carries many connotations, including, in certain contexts, that of frustration over, for example, perceived inequity in distribution of ceremonial goods. The person who gets angry too easily is also liable to become sick, they say, and this is because the family ghosts, looking down, may take pity on the person and send sickness as a means of marking them out for sympathy and redress. Looking at this from the outside, we can see that sickness can function as a means of protest, or at least attention-getting, much as possession by spirits can also be. Indeed, sickness may be thought of as resulting from such possession. Sickness is thus not just a passive condition but is an active role. In seeing things this way the Hagen people have gone further than the scientists who identified Type A personalities. They are saying that sickness and its treatment is an integral part of the process of control over feelings and relationships in their society. Their concept of anger and its link with sickness in fact provides the master pathway for understanding how they handle a range of conflicts and disputes between people. This example also, therefore, tells us something more: we cannot draw a line between what is "medical" and what is "legal." In the practice of social life, these spheres are intimately joined. The same is true for our own society: legal limits are set to medical practices having to do with, for example, conception on the one hand and death on the other, and with changing technologies these same limits become blurred and subject to much ethical debate. It is interesting, too, that such debates are often constrained by religious attitudes that are far more rigid than those we find in many tribal societies. Medical anthropology has to come to terms with these taboos of modern society. The whole controversy about surrogate parenting, for example, rests on a particular definition of kinship. It might surprise those involved in this argument to read about the various arrangements and definitions of parenthood made by the Nuer people of the Sudan in Africa, described a generation ago by the anthropologist Edward Evans-Pritchard (Evans-Pritchard 1951). Examples of this kind could serve to relativize and broaden the basis of ethical debates brought about by new medical technologies.

Another fundamental source for reflection on medical issues in our own society is provided by the philosopher of education Ivan Illich (Illich 1977). Illich argues against the removal from the individual of power over his or her own self and identity. He points to the "medicalization " of health issues which inevitably occurs as a result of the growth of medical knowledge and skill and the development of systems of both capitalist and socialized medical care in industrialized societies. For purposes of his argument, Illich stresses the phenomenon of iatrogenic sickness, the negative effects or side effects of medical practices. By this approach doctors are made almost to appear Machiavellian; but the more important analytical point is contained in his section on attitudes towards pain and suffering. Here we are dealing with worldviews and their influence on individual perceptions and on medical practice. This is a truly fascinating arena for research. Illich argues that whereas in Asian cultures medical practice developed with a strong inclination toward the relieving of pain, this was only incidental to Western medicine, which had more to do with the removal of pathogens. In contemporary Western society, however, a new twist has occurred with the development of readily available painkillers. Whereas in the past, and in other cultures—we may certainly cite the tribal societies again—the experience and endurance of pain has been an expected part of life and has in fact contributed to the dignity of the individual, Illich maintains, this self-respect is now removed by the endless prescription of painkilling drugs whose use further "medicalizes" the individual and is a symptom of the individual's exposure to medical professionals and the advertising industry. While his argument makes no sense when applied to acute conditions, whether temporary or terminal, or to conditions in which the relief of pain is also a genuine therapy as in medicines to relax muscle spasm, it does make rather powerful sense when applied to the prescription and sale of tranquilizers and pain relievers that may do nothing more than mask an underlying problem and create a dependency comparable to that on alcohol or nicotine. And once again the causes are sociogenic: "when you haven't got time for the pain" is one of the most telling refrains used in advertising a particular brand of painkiller on U.S. television. Busy people don't have time for headaches or other bodily pains. Society needs—indeed claims—their bodies even as they pursue an apparently individualist ethic of work or profit. And the painkilling industry closes the gap between individual performance and institutional demands. The perception and treatment of pain is thus fundamentally influenced by the politico-economic system.

This negative approach to health, however, has generated its dialectical opposite in the concept of "wellness" so popular nowadays. Naturally an industry also grows up around this idea in the United States. But in reaching towards it, the developed, industrialized world is once again only returning to a point long-since reached in tribal societies, the point where health, beauty, and political influence form a conglomerate. Everyone has seen pictures of New Guinea peoples, no doubt, dressed in colorful head dresses that may strike the viewers as the quintessence of the exotic. Yet in fact they are signs of wellness, of total well-being expressed at both the individual and the political level. The bright feathers and paint signify attractiveness, blessing by the ghosts, fertility, wealth, and above all "a good skin," the concept closest to our "health." New Guinea decorations combine in one complex the separate realms of fashion clothing, perfume, and health clinics in our society, welding these concerns into an integrated statement on the occasion of dance festivals (O'Hanlon 1989).

Returning from New Guinea to Pittsburgh once more, I want to say that the development of an interest in medical anthropology as a field of study makes a lot of sense for three interrelated reasons: first, this is a rapidly growing subdiscipline of anthropology within which theoretical ideas from the whole range of the subject can be brought into play. Second, it has an applied as well as a theoretical dimension, and funds can be sought for studies on the spot as well as in tribal or peasant cultures elsewhere. I would stress, though, that without its essential cross-cultural background and source of inspiration in ethnomedicine, medical anthropology would lose both its sense of fun and its long-term innovative power. Third, this field offers a genuine forum in which the old issues of the relationship between biological and cultural factors in the production of social processes can be reconsidered. It is to this general issue that I now also turn.

The State of the Art

In proposing that the pursuit of anthropology is a kind of odyssey, I do not mean to imply, of course, a point-by-point comparison between the peregrinations and tribulations of the wily Odysseus and the history of our subject. But I do mean to suggest that, like Odysseus, we have to keep our wits about us and that we are beset with various dangers, both political and intellectual. And while the truth, our beloved Penelope, may wait steadfastly for us, despite being importuned by unruly and greedy rival suitors, it is certainly not clear that we are about to sail in to the rocky shore of Ithaca and claim a well-deserved rest at last. Rather, we are still out on the wine-dark sea and subject from time to time to the violence of Polyphemus-like one-eyed theories as well as to the manipulative aestheticisms of Siren-sounding discourses and dialogues. In my introduction I indicated that anthropology is a journey in search equally of "the other" and of "ourselves." All problems of universality and particularity, as Marc Augé has pointed out (Augé 1982), revolve around these polarities. Inevitably, theories which base themselves on biological, psychological, or psychobiological principles tend to stress universality and by this either the identity of self and other or a linear measurement of other against self. By contrast, cultural anthropology practically came into being on a relativist ticket, the fact of diversity and the need to understand each culture in its own right or on its own terms. Structuralists attempt to overcome the polarity by elucidating common patterns of thought exhibited cross-culturally at an unconscious level; functionalists by arguing that diverse customs may serve identical functions; Marxists by referring everything to the mode of production; and sociobiologists by appealing first to Darwin and second to inclusive fitness as the prime mover of human affairs. It is practically inevitable, also, that biologists should march under the banner of science and cultural anthropologists should owe at least some lingering allegiance to the humanities— an allegiance that has recently recrudesced in the form of first hermeneutics and then postmodernist musings. What is necessary is some sense of balance in the midst of all this flux. The helpful side of the humanities connection is that it tells us we are dealing, as humans, with human values exhibited in history, and it warns us against naive neopositivist empiricism. It is less helpful, however, when it impels us into ever-deepening labyrinths of introspection and idiosyncrasy, in which we are likely to lose, rather than find, ourselves. Equally, on the scientific side, we can be inspired at least by the search for general propositions and rigorous methods without bowing down to the shibboleths of one-track oversimplification and hasty cross-inferences from animal to human studies. As an illustration, we may take one discipline that has grown up in this century with some promise towards anthropology: ethology, on which Robert Hinde, Royal Society Research Professor at the University of Cambridge, has published a series of attempts to show the relationship between this subject and the social sciences in general (Hinde 1987). Ethology starts from the naturalistic observation of behavioral patterns, attempting to relate these to genetic programs that generate fixed action patterns in response to releasing mechanisms. If there are such patterns for Homo sapiens, then clearly here is one basis for a universalist approach, whose significance will, however, depend on how important these patterns are in proportion to other influences on life and behavior in general. Hinde recognizes this question and argues that we need to distinguish three different levels: individuals, relationships, and culture. He also admits, at the outset, that superior cognitive ability and the invention of culture and language do clearly set humans off from other animals and that both human and animal behaviors are quite diverse. For humans, this diversity increases exponentially as a result of culture and social structure. Reformulating the categories of his book title, Hinde writes that we must distinguish between interactions, relationships, and social structure, and we must see that there are two-way relations between these levels, as well as dialectical relations between behavior at all levels and the environment. Hinde warns that "a search for direct links between particular human dispositions and human social practices, institutions or beliefs, is unlikely to be rewarding" (1987:27). This is surely sound advice, but when biologists enter the field of cultural studies they unfortunately tend to do exactly what Hinde here cautions against. His own recommendation that one should look at influences between different levels and his mention of the term dialectics in this context both point the way to a much more complicated world. Later in his book, after listing a number of apparently universal individual characteristics, he takes on the question of sex differences in cognitive abilities, citing as an example the fact that in Britain girls from the age of about eleven years on tend not to perform as well in mathematics in secondary schools as boys (1987:141). Hinde agrees that this is partly a result of teachers' expectations based on gender stereotypes, but he cites other research attributing superior spatial visualization to boys rather than girls. And he thinks that "it remains a real possibility that the stereotype is linked to very small mean differences, which are then exaggerated because it is in the interests of one or the other party to do so" (1987:142). This is an example of what he calls dialectical relations between levels. Exaggeration, however, is not a kind of dialectics. Further, if it is to be explained by interests, then it is to these that we need to direct attention at the appropriate level. The biological substratum appears here to be considerably less significant than the level of social relations and politics.

Thus Hinde's own cautionary dictum proves to be particularly true in the case of this example. He himself still concludes that it is important to know that there is a biological basis for the stereotype, because "an understanding of how the stereotype develops may help us to change it." Unfortunately, it may also be counterproductive, as Hinde admits, because "to acknowledge their possible existence contributes to the reality of the stereotype" (1987:142). The same holds for many other debates, such as that on human aggression. Finally, on inclusive fitness as an explanation for all and sundry behavior, Hinde points out that an institution such as initiation has complex functions and may enhance inclusive fitness in one respect while having neutral or deleterious consequences for such fitness in other respects. Recognition of this possibility follows from his conceptualization of group structure and sociocultural structure as separate domains from the levels of the individual and dyadic relationships.

Overall, Hinde clearly believes in the utility of the approach through ethology (and also ecology). But he is equally clearly aware of its limitations, and his acknowledgment of levels practically leaves sociocultural anthropology intact. His own brief venture into dialectics ends without any dialectics demonstrated; but what he certainly has shown is that using the ideas derived from ethology one can *ask* a range of questions which otherwise would not be asked. In other words, one can set out on a new part of the journey that is anthropology's odyssey. The danger for ethologists is that they will jump from primates to sociological data on Western societies without really using the huge register of ethnological information we now have. Ethology then turns back into ideology.

The mention of ideology here, as well as the example of sex differences, indicates that there is another pressing part of the journey that has to be faced by today's anthropologist, and that is the political context of one's work. This is not just a problem of where to find a field area, but one of what to do with the information collected. Since the 1970s there have been severe critiques mounted of anthropologists, most notably by Marxists who questioned the collaboration of anthropologists with colonial and imperialist regimes throughout the world, or even claimed that all of the concepts of anthropology were emic artifacts of bourgeois ideology. This phase of the attack has now died down. But out of it a new— and, to me, paradoxical—situation has emerged. One product of the Marxist review of anthropology was a demand for more re- flexivity and an abandonment of the pseudo-anonymity of the ethnographer in the ethnography. One result was a spate of auto- biographical accounts of work in the field. These remain to be re- viewed critically and comprehensively as yet, but they are certainly a welcome addition to the corpus of ethnography. But, at a slightly more remote extension, this demand for reflexivity has further fed into a kind of literary anti-objectivism, and this in turn into a full-blown postmodernism that sees anthropology more as poetics than as science. The apotheosis or *reductio ad absurdum* of this approach is found in Stephen Tyler's book *The Unspeakable: Discourse, Dialogue and Rhetoric in the Post-Modern World* (1987), where he protests against all texts as killers of speech and sug- gests that a postmodern ethnography would be "a co-operatively evolved text consisting of fragments of discourse intended to evoke . . . an emergent fantasy of a possible world of common sense reality and thus to provoke an aesthetic integration that will have a therapeutic effect" (202). What this strange beast would look like is as yet unclear—partly because even Stephen Tyler does not claim to know how to write an ethnography in this way. As a concept, this appears to be the historical antithesis of holism— perhaps "fragmentism"! However that may be, this version of the postmodernist quest is one I cannot fully share, preferring, rather, to return to the earlier and more fruitful point that was reached already in the 1960s with the call for reflexivity. The retreats into texts, introspection, a literary style, admission of multiple uncer- tainties and ambiguities are all in a sense products of a loss of nerve in the face of Marxist-inspired critiques of our subject. Func- tionalist monographs were derided, correctly, but also with the aim of denigrating the fieldwork process that produced them. Taking information from texts was seen as less morally culpable than making texts by writing down what people say and do. But this is absurd, because unless someone does primary research how can such secondary inspection of texts take place? Two neg- atives do not make a positive in this case, and the denial of both functionalism *and* fieldwork leaves anthropology without its essential tool of progress, its excitement, and its challenge to do *new kinds* of fieldwork or to do fieldwork in *new places*. That the political context today is utterly different from that of Africa in the 1940s or the Pacific in the 1960s is thoroughly obvious. I, for example, have spent ten years of my professional life teaching anthropology and subsequently running a program of cultural research in the country where my fieldwork has been done over a period of time that spanned the transition to independence and the consolidation of the independent State of Papua New Guinea. During these years, 1973–77 and 1981–86, I encountered innumerable examples of both hostility toward ethnographic work and great appreciation for it, and I remain absolutely convinced of the importance of the subject there, where the studies have been done, as much as here, where we spend our time talking about them at a distance. By the same token, studies carried out here, in medical anthropology, for example, using insights derived from elsewhere, could make a real contribution to the society that funds them. The answer to our problems as anthropologists today is not, therefore, to retreat into the illusory safety of texts and save ourselves from the awkward problems of fieldwork—a condition I would liken to being in the land of the Lotus-Eaters—but to get our boats out again into the sea and master its choppy waves, blown as they are by political winds around the globe. First-hand experience, for all that it gives no epistemological or ethical privilege, is absolutely indispensable to a lively and rounded understanding of any part of the world. Equally, it does not guarantee successful theorizing. Anthropology needs both its Marcel Mauss and its Bronislaw Malinowski.

I aim these remarks particularly toward younger anthropologists, who now enter the subject at a time when values appear to be thrown into confusion. Anthropology is truly an inspiring subject, and we should not be discouraged by fears of shrinking field areas, fingers of accusation, or doubts about the future of theory. We are not forced to be either universalists or particularists. Still less do we have to give way to the latest attempts to transform our subject into something else; rather, these other disciplines or ideas should be made to contribute to our own endeavors (Marcus and Fischer 1986). Let us, then, take to ourselves the spirit of Odysseus and sail wherever the winds blow, but let us steer the boat where *we* want it to go.

References

Augé, Marc
    1982 *The Anthropological Circle.* Cambridge University Press, Cambridge.
Bailey, Frederick G.
    1977 *Morality and Expediency: The Folklore of Academic Politics.* Basil Blackwell, London.
Douglas, Mary
    1966 *Purity and Danger.* Routledge and Kegan Paul, London.
    1970 *Natural Symbols.* Vintage Press, New York.
Evans-Pritchard, Edward E.
    1951 *Kinship and Marriage among the Nuer.* Clarendon Press, Oxford.
Fabrega, Horacio, Jr.
    1974 *Disease and Social Behavior: An Interdisciplinary Perspective.* MIT Press, Cambridge, Mass.
Hinde, Robert A.
    1987 *Individuals, Relationships and Culture: Links between Ethology and the Social Sciences.* Cambridge University Press, Cambridge.
Illich, Ivan
    1977 *Limits to Medicine, Medical Nemesis: The Expropriation of Health.* Pelican Books, London.
Lock, Margaret, and Nancy Scheper-Hughes
    1987 The Mindful Body: A Prolegomenon to Future Work in Medical Anthropology. *Medical Anthropology Quarterly* 1(1):6–41.
Marcus, George, and Michael M. Fischer
    1986 *Anthropology as Cultural Critique: An Experimental Moment in the Human Sciences.* University of Chicago Press, Chicago.
O'Hanlon, Michael
    1989 *Reading the Skin.* British Museum Publications, London.
Strathern, Andrew J.
    1979 *Ongka: A Self-Account by a New Guinea Big-Man.* Gerald Duckworth, London.
Tyler, Stephen A.
    1987 *The Unspeakable: Discourse, Dialogue and Rhetoric in the Post-Modern World.* University of Wisconsin Press, Madison.

SEVEN

Reconstructing Anthropology

1990

Since the 1960s we have experienced a series of books that has attempted to redefine anthropology. Edmund Leach (1961), for example, announced to us that we must "rethink" the subject; more radically, Dell Hymes (1969) urged that it should be veritably "re-invented." Such trends of thought can be seen as tentative precursors of the movement that began to swirl around us in the mid-1980s, the declaration that our discipline should not be re-thought but de-thought, or "deconstructed."

At first sight this curious metaphor, with its imprecise image of either tearing down or meticulously dismantling a building, might seem to correspond only to the laudable aim of further analyzing our topics in order to find new ways of approaching them. This technique of thought, of course, is by no means new, but it usually has the implied further aim of rebuilding the same topics on a rearranged basis. Indeed, much of the valuable "precursor" work of the 1960s and 1970s in anthropology was precisely of this sort. Necessarily, what is certain has to be made uncertain before a different pattern can be established. However, deconstructionism, with that baneful generalizing suffix added, intends much more than straightforward reanalysis. It involves the dissolution of all that we know and our release into a kind of perpetual mist in which signifiers playfully chase signifieds in a game of tag but without any real intention of finding them, or any notion that it really matters or is possible to do so—a sort of perpetually unresolved blindman's buff. If this supposedly creative game is designed, as it claims, to bring us into a new era of meta-

The material for this chapter is from a lecture given in the Distinguished Speakers series at the University of Pittsburgh Johnstown Campus, in February 1990.

ethnography, we have to ask ourselves what the creature is, in this curious afterworld of postmodernism, this dimly Elysian fin-de-siècle reverie, that apparently now "slouches towards Bethlehem to be born" in that context where "things fall apart," "the center cannot hold," and "the falcon cannot hear the falconer" (W. B. Yeats, "The Second Coming").

Several streams of ideas have converged toward the current of postmodernism, many of them brilliantly caricatured in Malcolm Bradbury's vignette *Mensonge* (1987). In social anthropology alone the procession from structural-functionalism to structuralism to poststructuralism is one stream; another was the development of transactionalism and ethnomethodology, with their emphasis on negotiated exchanges of meaning; a third moves from classical Marxism to neo-Marxism to structural Marxism, and then blends with poststructuralism. Still the nagging question remains: in the midst of many -isms, are we getting anywhere? And what are the post-structures being invoked? Are they new structures or just a recognition of non-structure?

If we wish to find something positive here, it is worthwhile to recall a pattern that emerged from the effort to "reinvent" anthropology and bring it away from the pseudo-objectivist stance of naive empiricism: the pattern of reflexivity or, more broadly, reflectiveness. Essentially, this means questioning our own categories of thought, treating ourselves as objects of study, as well as the people "out there," and realizing that the construction of knowledge means building a bridge from two ends at once and calculating hopefully that the parts will meet in the middle. Meta-ethnography, if it means anything worthwhile, has to chart and direct that process of bridge building, but if so it is no longer a matter of deconstruction but of reconstruction. And this, in fact, is what we should be doing today. The exercise, as you can imagine, is by no means easy; but it is usually easier to take things apart than to put them together again.

Let me first try, then, to summarize what I think is valuable in postmodernist thought and then proceed to use it in ways that will help us to reconstruct certain categories of thought in anthropology and to re-illuminate the sorts of perennial problems with which we have been wrestling since anthropology became a professional academic subject. Putting things very baldly, the useful aspects of this intellectual fashion show appear to be the following: (1) our faith in the certainty of received truths is once more thoroughly shaken; (2) we are forced to become flexible in our approach to thinking; (3) we are compelled to be cautious and skeptical about the very use of language as a means of objective communication between persons; and (4) the rhetorical assertion that old connections cannot be made makes us think harder of new connections which perhaps can. As is clear, these virtues are rather minor, in the sense that they are all negative or preliminary, unless we want to release ourselves finally into an apocalyptic "cloud of unknowing," or squeeze ourselves flat into the text of a library book and remain there folded away. In themselves these positivities are no more than warning signs that tell us to be careful in our trade.

Perhaps you will think this is unfair. If so, let me give here a sketch of the ideas of Stephen Tyler, who has become a kind of guru-scribe for postmodernism in anthropology and has recently published his manifesto for postmodern ethnography in the final chapter of his 1987 book *The Unspeakable* (an awkward title, perhaps intendedly so, see Kirby 1989). According to the description at the back of this book, Tyler's aim is one which ought to be desirable, that of returning us to "the everyday common sense environments of oral discourse," and so recovering for us "the oral world through writing rather than through the deconstruction of writing." If he can do this, it will surely be another step in making anthropology less alienated, more unified with its object of discourse and, in that sense, more relevant. Tyler would in fact be creating a post-postmodernist stance, which really would be a reconstruction and would call out for its own name among names, perhaps "neopragmatism." If this is so, however, why does Tyler seek to make a transition, as he says, from ethnography as "document of the occult" to it as "occult document"? What is this notion that it is excellent to make things hard to understand? Clearly, it is the result of ambition, an ambition similar in principle to that which led the British social anthropologist Evans-Pritchard at the end of his first book on the Nuer people of the Sudan to write that we should try to find "relations between relations," a superordinate or metastructure beyond the empirical structure of clans, tribes, villages, and lineage segments that he had been describing with such meticulous care in the preceding 200 pages (Evans-Pritchard 1940). It was an ambition similar also to that of Lévi-Strauss, who in placing metaphor on metonym and reading from one level to another in his analyses of "savage thought" (or "wild pansies") and mythology, in particular, certainly was reaching for the relations between relations which Evans-Pritchard had only perceived should, in principle, be there without ever grasping what they were. However, as arcane as Lévi-Strauss's thought sometimes is, it is not so baffling as Tyler's, whose prose sometimes takes on a tortuous and incantatory aura. He declares that ethnography is transcendent, and that in it all other discourses (for example, those of science and politics) are relativized and "find their meaning and justification." How is ethnography going to do this? In *The Unspeakable* Tyler goes to some length to deny all the ways we might have thought of: "Transcendent, then, neither by theory nor by practice, nor by their synthesis, it *describes* no knowledge and *produces* no action. It transcends instead by *evoking* what cannot be known discursively or performed perfectly, though all know it as if discursively and perform it as if perfectly." And if we ask what this central activity of evocation—or the calling up of things—is, he tells us again what it is not: "Evocation is neither presentation nor representation. It presents no objects and represents none, yet it makes available through absence what can be conceived but not presented. It is thus beyond truth and immune to the judgment of performance" (1987:199).

And Tyler, continuing in this oddly mystical—not to say Old Testament–like—way, also announces to us the death of science as well as the birth of the "new ethnography": "Evocation—that is to say, ethnography—is the discourse of the post-modern world, for the world that made science, and that scientific thought made is now an archaic mode of consciousness surviving for awhile yet in degraded form without the ethnographic context that created and sustained it" (200).

Wishful thinking, perhaps, on Tyler's part. The symbol of science has indeed been overused in anthropology to beat down tendencies towards humanism. But Tyler's own foghorn rhetoric only reverberates in the mist. It is in a sense the linguistic model gone mad, reducing science and everything else to words and language rather than genuine discoveries. It becomes "curiouser and curiouser," given the extraordinary progress that is being made in certain branches of sciences founded precisely on that creative rethinking of categories that the positive side of postmodernism recommends. I am thinking here of psychobiology and its growing reconceptualization of the relationship between the mind and the body, a trend which I believe gives us a chance also to reconstruct the body of theory in anthropology rather than dissect it and throw it away as outdated.

In chapter six I quoted Tyler's definition of what a postmodern ethnography is, chiefly in order to point out how quirky the whole thing is. Perhaps it will bear quoting again: "A post-modern ethnography is a cooperatively evolved text consisting of fragments of discourse intended to evoke in the minds of both reader and writer an emergent fantasy of a possible world of common sense reality, and thus to provoke an aesthetic integration that will have a therapeutic effect" (1987:202).

Apart from the stipulations that the text be "cooperatively evolved" and that its discourse has to be in "fragments," this actually sounds quite like some of the better science fiction works, especially those of Ursula K. Le Guin, for example her early book *The Lathe of Heaven* (1973) and her later one *Always Coming Home* (1986) which is explicitly cast as an ethnography. And indeed, today we are well aware that the categories of ethnography and fiction have an area of overlap, within which the concept of evocation probably finds its proper place (Jackson 1989). Further, it is healthy to admit that ethnography aims at having a rhetorical or persuasive point or, if you like, at arguing a case and thus providing a sort of "therapy," as Tyler puts it. Finally, it is by now a familiar point that one of the functions of ethnography is to "defamiliarize the familiar" as well as the reverse. Indeed, every attempt to conceptualize "the other" is encapsulated simultaneously in an attempt to reconceptualize ourselves. Tyler has, in an odd way, completed the circle of that thought by telling us that his ethnography is nothing other than the old concept of poetry given a dialogical twist so that "a story of sorts" is produced, one which

Tyler suddenly compares to the stories found in the Bible (1987:204) and which, he says, evokes a "participatory reality" constructed by ethnographer and informants together. He also says that this as-yet-to-be ethnography will avoid grounding itself "in the theoretical and common sense categories of the hegemonic western tradition" (206). Tyler continues relentlessly to tell us what this ethnography will not be and will not do and in doing so dances past the already accepted postmodernisms of Derrida and Company, creating out of this new imagined construction a veritable will-o'-the-wisp, or wisp (maybe warp)-o'-the-will, something anarchic that refuses to be ruled or to be subject to what he calls "that parody of scientific scrutiny known as criticism" (206). One can only comment that this is a quick evasive tactic that does not deserve to be subjected even to a parody of criticism. While Tyler's attack on naive scientific realism—with its jargon of facts, hypotheses, and experiments all borrowed from physics—is well taken, his self-abandonment into the arms of mysticism hardly gives us a glimpse of what in practice we should be doing beyond suggesting that we talk a lot and let others do the same and see if anything comes out of this exercise. Like myself, Tyler recognizes that deconstruction has merely deconstructed without instructing us or constructing anything. However, he appears to assume that if the modernist project has been reduced to rubble, the parts needed to make anything coherent are now missing and we have to make do with fragments, a consideration he justifies by pointing out that "life in the field is itself fragmentary" (208) and that the postmodern consciousness is itself a fragmentary one since there is for us no "synthesizing allegory" and therefore no "aesthetic totalization." Pleasure, then, we can have, but only in little pieces— tessellae that do not compose a scene—because that would be representational, and Tyler says that the new ethnography must not represent things but only be a discourse, one which will not synthesize oppositions into transcendent propositions but evoke transcendence outside itself. In short, it will be an incantation that will release the genie from the bottle, but we have so far not the faintest clue what this genie will be, except that somehow it will look like ourselves perhaps eating a piece of bread, staring into a mirror, or musing as we step on or off a bus. It will be like what we already are, only thinking more, and we will feel happier as a result of it. Tyler claims that it will "depart from the common sense world only in order to reconfirm it and to return us to it renewed and mindful of our renewal" (211). It will be like a charismatic religious experience, then, though Tyler denies that there can be anymore a religious form of transcendence. Tyler's recipe looks much like the aims of some of the Japanese New Religions, in fact, since he argues that its intent is "to reassimilate, to reintegrate the self in society and to restructure the conduct of everyday life" (212). Overall, my suspicion is that Tyler has delivered ethnography out of the hands of scientists and critics, literary or other, into those of the novelists and has finally closed the gap between ethnography and fiction. Those who can't write novels won't be ethnographers in the future. Nor will they truly have had "experience," it seems, since only in writing the ethnography will the experience take shape (215).

Tyler's final words out of the unresolved polyphony of his own propositions are peculiarly like the ending of Evans-Pritchard's book on the Nuer or David Schneider's *A Critique of the Concept of Kinship* (1984): "I call ethnography a meditative vehicle because we come to it not as to a map of knowledge nor as a guide to action, nor even for entertainment. We come to it as the start of a different kind of journey" (216).

Perhaps the best way to describe this nonprogrammatic program for ethnography is that it apocalyptically announces that there is no apocalypse. It is like a tremendously condensed black-hole form of emics that collapses inwardly and becomes a description so "thick," in Geertz's terms, that we cannot see through it at all. As I read it, then, Tyler's idea only seems to go beyond the methodological negativities of standard postmodernism. He offers us a vision, which turns out to be banal—perhaps a postmodernist joke, then, the demon of irony, announcing with glee that of course we should have known all along that the snark was really a boojum, you see.

I have mentioned an area of investigation that I think shows a very genuine promise of insight both for anthropology and for everyday life and one which returns us, too, to the commonsense worlds of both ourselves and those we study in far-flung parts of the world. This is the new synthesis of ideas emerging within medical anthropology that, considered in full, literally gives us a new picture of ourselves as humanity. It involves a reconceptualization of the mind-body dichotomy, the Cartesian split that produced the categories of "rationality" versus "emotionality," on which Western biomedicine has initially taken its stand and which we now find calls out for a genuine synthetic transcendence in order simply to explain what happens in practice. In a turn similar to that which Tyler makes back to the world of the so-called primitives, we are finding that there is such an intimate connection between the mind and the body that it is much better to dissolve these as separate categories and look at holistic interrelationships, at gestalt phenomena. Strange that no indigenous New Guinean would ever have doubted that proposition, although he or she would express it in different terms. But to acknowledge the enormous insight of other cultures does not mean we have to abandon the scientific traditions of our own. The exciting feature of the development of ideas today is that the neurophysiology of the brain literally enables us to see how the connections are made within us that produce the gestalt which we are. Yet, at the same time, these biologically oriented findings do not replace or get rid of the problems of culture and society, of how entities enter a social and cultural matrix and are there handled in contexts of solidarity, conflict, power, exploitation, and negotiation. There are, therefore, two sides to this new anthropology, but both center on the idea or metaphor of the "body." One side is the work in "critical" medical anthropology done by Margaret Lock and Nancy Scheper-Hughes. In their paper "The Mindful Body" (1987), these two authors pointed out that instead of relying on the old idea of the separation of mind and body we must now conceptualize the idea of the body in the political, the social, the cultural, and the individual realms, and we must understand that each person's "body"—we could rephrase this as "each person as a mind-body amalgam"—is implicated in all of these different levels and in one way or another expresses them by its condition. Through all the levels of implication there is a co-association of physicality and meaning. We do not exit from physicality at the cultural level nor from meaning at the individual level. The formulation here is reminiscent of Victor Turner's arguments regarding ritual, which he saw as having both a sensory, or visceral, pole and a pole of rationality. Symbols used in ritual were multivocalic and contained elements of both poles. The new neurobiology, which Turner himself was studying shortly before his death, can tell us why; or rather, it can show us how this actually operates, without explaining the orders that are constructed in social relations themselves. These are orders into which contested images of the body enter and are themselves made the object of struggles. One need go no further than the debate regarding the pros and cons of abortion that rages in America today and the more subdued but equally urgent arguments regarding surrogate parenting to realize that this is actually true, and it is important to realize that these are arguments about the body that can never be resolved by regarding them as scientific or pseudo-scientific statements alone. The question "When does life begin?" is inherently enigmatic and contestable and subject to cross-cultural variation, and different cosmological answers to it might lead either to a taboo on eating certain plants and vegetables on the Pythagorean principle that they might enclose transmigrated souls or to the custom of consuming the bodies of dead infants as a means of passing on messages to the gods! A scientific knowledge of conception does not settle these debates immediately, as one might otherwise suppose, because the body which is being thought of in these debates is not only the biological body but the body politic, a tool for contesting actions constructed within opposed historical traditions and in terms of which factions crystallize and reform over time. In a sense, Tyler's characterization of the postmodern condition as being one without a synthesizing allegory applies here. Such allegories define boundaries: when life begins/can begin or ends/can end. Without them the boundaries become contested and subject to uncertainty, especially if technological changes alter the conditions of operation of the boundaries in question. Factions then claim false metonymy for themselves and struggles ensue. That the debates should be particularly marked in the United States is a reflection of the peculiar dialectical tension here between the ideology of the democratic state, in which law rules, and the ideology of individual free will, in which the person has maximum control over his or her own affairs.

I give this example as a brief demonstration of the applicability of the ideas of Lock and Scheper-Hughes. Underlying the intensity of debate, however, is the fact I stressed: in the last analysis, debates are about the body, something everyone has and intimately experiences, and therefore the cathexis between arguments and feelings is bound to be particularly strong. Neurobiology, as I have said, is showing us exactly *how* this kind of cathexis takes place, and the key lies in studying the relevant interconnections of parts of the brain. This same model of relationships also shows us how emotional states are linked to social relationships and emerge in conditions of health and sickness. The new medical anthropology, therefore, aims to link all of these spheres together in a coherent form of discourse that can enrich greatly the understanding we have of ourselves and others around us. But the first essential step is to get an idea of linkages within the brain itself between its reptilian (brain stem), old mammalian (limbic-hypothalamic-pituitary), and new mammalian (neocortical) parts. It is within the old mammalian part that the trophotropic maintenance functions belonging to the parasympathetic nervous system have their location, in balance with the ergotropic functions of the sympathetic nervous system. In terms of the right and left division between cerebral hemispheres of the brain connected by the corpus callosum, the trophotropic function, which has a calming effect on the person, belongs to the nondominant, or right, hemisphere and the ergotropic to the left hemisphere, which also controls analytical ability, the use of propositional language, and the recognition of temporarity. Victor Turner has taken all this and raised the question of how the brain functions in ritual states, whether the religious symbols which are activated in ritual gain force not only from the semantic meaning imputed to them by the operation of the left hemispherical cortex but also from emotional seats in older parts of the brain associated with the right hemisphere. In so doing he has found a way back to his earlier problem of the two poles of meanings in ritual symbols and forwards into a theory of neurobiological tuning which is relevant to the explanation of trance.

The implication overall is that there is a definite line of connection between the neocortex (which we might label "mind") and the limbic-hypothalamic complex (Turner 1985:252ff). As Rossi notes in his book *The Psychobiology of Mind-Body Healing* (1986), endocrinologists explain that under pressure "the limbic-hypothalamic system in the brain converts the neural messages of mind into the neuro-hormonal messenger molecules of the body" (xiv). This is the start of a chain of communication that reaches ultimately to the immune system and its responses to health and sickness. Combining Rossi's explanation with Turner's problem of ritual symbols, we may note how often the African rituals of the Ndembu people whom Turner studied had specifically to do with the question of sickness and its healing. If under the trance-like conditions produced by these rituals the neocortically transmitted messages could penetrate more effectively (i.e., with less resistance) to the immune system, we would have an explanation of why ritual symbols could work to speed up the processes of healing in afflicted persons.

Perception of factors of this kind in fact enables us to explain many things which otherwise remain inexplicable, mysterious, and contested on the peripheries of the biomedical model of disease control. As happens at times of revolution in science or politics, what was once peripheral or suppressed becomes central and the source of a new paradigm. Rossi quotes tellingly from Norman Cousins, "the placebo is the doctor who resides within," and he comments that "this statement reflects a profound change from the traditional view of the placebo as a nuisance factor" (1986:15).

Rossi goes on to introduce a number of new synthesizing concepts that enable us to reconceptualize the mind-body problem as a whole and therefore see how interactions between mind and body can produce healing or, by the same token, sickness. The major import of these concepts is that instead of thinking of mind and body as separate entities we have to understand them as parts of an overall information system in which hormones, neurotransmitters, and also neuropeptides are seen as operating at the molecular level to convey informational messages which modify the state of the system as a whole. It is important here that Rossi seems to give some primacy to the mind as a "moving agent" which produces original messages that are then transduced or translated by molecular forms of action into the body. This conception of "mind" is what provides a linkage point between his work and that of anthropologists, for, as his case histories make abundantly clear, it is social relationships that are the context in which thoughts and moods that get translated into the state of the body originate. The body thus becomes the image of these social relationships, and the study of the body becomes the study of the effects of society upon the individual.

Another notable feature of Rossi's approach, which underlies the therapy he has practiced along with the psychologist Milton Erickson, is his positive view of the unconscious. This is in stark contrast to Freud's view of the unconscious id and superego, the sources of libido and punishment, and is the reason why Rossi considers that hypnosis gives therapist and patient access to the potentially creative powers of the unconscious brain located within the right hemisphere. Problems also exist at this level which are the product of state-dependent memory and learning, another important concept Rossi employs. Human learning in general is state-dependent and in some instances strongly so, such that recall can only be effected when the original frame in which the learning took place is recreated. Memory itself is not a simple retrieval of stored knowledge, but is creative reframing; again, the gestalt abilities of the right hemisphere are implicated. This same capacity for reframing is what enables the therapist to assist the patient in converting symptoms of physical pain or illness first into signals and then into pointers for the refashioning of life. Dreams can be used in the same way, as indicators of pathways towards healing.

Most of Rossi's effort is concentrated on showing the state of research on the actual molecular processes which make the links between body and mind and therefore constitute the new psychobiology. Particularly intriguing is his report that the neuropeptide system may affect more general processes within the body than was hitherto thought, enabling, for example, the immune and endocrine systems "to communicate with each other by virtue of signal molecules (hormones) and receptors common to both systems" (1986:187). But in addition to the attention he pays to the ever-deepening knowledge of the molecular level, Rossi also realizes that his theme and the findings to date do have much relevance for anthropology. In his chapter on mind modulation of the immune system, he stresses again the impact of information theory on our concept of the mind-body continuum and introduces the notion of information as inversely related to probability. Information is that which is new and unexpected and so can form the basis for a different level of awareness. This point in turn enables us to understand better one aspect of medical pluralism, thus:

> This is probably the reason why patients who have not found help by conventional medicine intuitively turn to the unusual and often seemingly bizarre approaches of other cultures and holistic medicine. . . . The unusual practices of the mystery religions and foreign healers break through the constricting and deadening effect of the familiar to access and activate the high information value of the new within the body-mind of the patients. (Rossi 1986:180–181).

And more generally still, Rossi notes: "This integration of previously separate studies in fields as diverse as philosophy, religion, cultural anthropology, psychology, biology, neurology, and molecular genetics is precisely what is most valuable in our developing information theory of mind-body healing" (181).

Thus we are able to retrieve for the world of scientific discussion the actions of shamans and healers which otherwise would simply be instances of exotic practices or irrationality. The circle of thought is closed, since the latest scientific thinking now begins to converge with that of the shaman or medicine man while offering in fact an explanation of why it is that shamanic healing does sometimes work. An example that occurs in Rossi's account is his discussion of the enteric system. It is a well-known fact that in many cultures important aspects of feeling are supposedly located in the stomach. This is a concept, for example, that has leading force in Japanese ideas about sickness. It is also found in both the Highlands cultures of Papua New Guinea with which I have carried out fieldwork, the Melpa and Wiru. It appears that the stomach's condition is used most often to express emotional discomfort (in Melpa *kitim kit enem*, in Wiru *tepe pooko*, both meaning "the stomach is bad"). Rossi confirms that this cross-cultural emphasis is by no means accidental, since "when we are emotionally upset . . . the entire gastrointestinal tract can express our discomfort. The sensitivity of the gastrointestinal tract to mental stress is one of the most widely recognized manifestations of psychosomatic problems" (1986:188). Concern for the stomach, then, is to be expected in ethnomedical systems around the world.

Melpa ideas about sickness also provide us with another parallel to the universal concepts suggested by Rossi. It is a Melpa belief that sickness can result from anger, *popokl*, which emerges in the *noman*, a metaphorical organ located in the chest which serves as a kind of barometer of the person's overall condition. Sickness can be cured if the person recognizes the anger that has caused it and confesses this, thus getting rid of it and enabling themselves to get better. Without appearing too fanciful, one can here make a direct translation from Melpa to Rossi's concepts.

Melpa	*Rossi*
Sickness results from a condition of the *noman*.	Sickness results from action in the limbic-hypothalamic system.
Specifically it comes from anger.	It may come from an unfavorable state-dependent learning experience.
It is cured when the anger is removed by confession.	It can be cured by accessing memory through hypnosis and by creative reframing of the experience as a signal rather than a symptom.

Of course, the worldviews and imagery are markedly different in the two cases, but the correspondence is still there.

There is also a correspondence that can be detected between Rossi's argument concerning the gestalt functions of the right hemisphere of the brain in assisting the process of healing and the form taken by Melpa curing spells. These are invariably metaphorical, creating images of a striking or unusual kind that project a sense of the desired cure upon the patient. Apart from the obvious logic involved, the significance of this fact lies precisely in the mobilization of emotional resources which is thereby effected for the patients. Rather than the spell acting mechanically on the sick person's condition, we have to see it acting holistically *with* the sick person in order to produce a healing. The approach via psychobiology therefore enables us to improve our ethnographic theory of the efficacy of spells.

Finally, Rossi's theory of the functions of the right cerebral hemisphere can be compared with Turner's theory of the production of trance in ritual. I referred earlier to Turner's idea of neurobiological tuning. Such tuning is thought to occur as a result of certain stimuli, notably sonic, visual, or photic driving, which initially excite the ergotropic side and eventually spill over into the trophotropic, at which point trance ensues with mixed discharges from both sides of the brain. Turner further suggests that the end results of both meditation and ritual may be the same, to wit an experience of the union of binary opposites which are maintained so clearly by the left side of the brain normally, and "an emergent awareness of polar opposites as presented in myth, [which now] appear simultaneously *both* as antinomies and as unified wholes" (1985:261). One might think of this as the brain realizing its own unity, which ordinarily is denied to it, an apotheosis of the corpus callosum that links left to right. The experience of transcendence or of what cannot be expressed, the ineffable, would then be a product of this experience of union, like the Platonic theory of Love or the Christian notion of making whole what was broken.

In a strange and unpredictable way we here return full circle to some of the pronouncements made *ex cathedra* by Tyler in his idiosyncratic postmodernist vision of ethnography; and on this return we can make sense out of what is otherwise baffling in his arcane pronouncements. For Tyler too speaks of the ineffable as the final aim of the peculiar discourse that he sees ethnography to be, so full of meaning that in the end this cannot be expressed. The postmodern ethnography, he says, "Will be a text of the physical, the spoken, and the performed, an evocation of quotidian experience, a palpable reality that uses everyday speech to suggest what is ineffable, not through abstraction, but by means of the concrete" (1987:213).

The quasi-religious overtones in Tyler's textual voice here alert us to the fact that he too is seeking transcendence, and his final proposition confirms this when he states that he calls ethnography "a meditative vehicle" (216), just as it was presaged when he earlier declared it to be ritual poetry (202). From our trek away from Tyler's postmodern, but somehow medieval, obscurantism and into the theorizing of Turner and Rossi on psychobiology, healing, and ritual, we are able to turn back to Tyler and see in what sense he wants ethnography to be poetry, meditation, therapy. It is simply that his own text has become a ritual text, a statement of belief which therefore inevitably takes on a transcendental tone. His text can thus be explained and classified, something that would be an anathema to him; it allows us to see postmodernism as another kind of paradoxical salvation cult, an apotheosis without a theos.

In this discussion I, by contrast, have not been concerned with invoking any *deus ex machina* as the final explanation of all things. I have attempted to indicate, however, that a powerful combination of ideas can be made for anthropology in general by joining together what we know from medical anthropology about cross-cultural theories of the body and sickness and the findings of psychobiology regarding neurohormonal receptors and message bearers. In this regard we may argue that a genuine breakthrough in cognitive studies can be achieved by concentrating not only on the logical properties of "mind" as shown in the work of the left hemisphere of the brain, but also on the gestalt "body image" qualities of the right hemisphere and on emergent findings regarding the interrelationship between the hemispheres. This can enable us to do what has been said of the Greek tragic poet Sophocles, that "He saw life steadily and saw it whole."

The viewpoints I have here expressed are comparable with those of Michael Jackson, for example, who, with respect to the concept of ethnographic truth, writes:

The deep disquiet felt by many scientists over the invasion of their domain by fictional and interpretive styles is, like the traditionally defensive attitude of artists towards science, good evidence that these discourses can never really isolate themselves from each other. Though they vie for dominance perhaps, like quarrelling lovers, the truth is they cannot exist without each other (1989:77).

Two remarkable chapters in Jackson's *Paths toward a Clearing* also resonate strongly with my argument: entitled "Knowledge of the Body" (chap. 8) and "Thinking through the Body" (chap. 9). In the first, Jackson writes of the way in which much effective knowledge in pragmatic activities is encoded nonverbally in bodily routines and skill, and this same kind of encoding appears also in ritual. In the second, he makes explicit reference to the kinds of cosmic analogies with the human body made in many cultures and to the therapeutic value of metaphor and poetry as a means of reforging wholeness of Being.

One of the drawbacks of much modern medicine is its reluctance to range over *all* the domains of Being—personal, social, natural—in diagnostic and therapeutic work. A kind of absolutism prevails in which specific symptoms are assigned determinate causes and doctors pour scorn on the opportunistic character of "alternative" or "primitive" medicine. Such doctrinal inflexibility undoubtedly reflects the fact that metaphor is no longer a key instrumentality in modern medical practice. Yet, as we have seen, it is by facilitating movement within the total field of Being that metaphor is a crucial means of locating areas where we can act upon those areas where we have lost the power to act. Insofar as modern medicine makes the doctor the sole actor in diagnostic and therapeutic practice, the devalorization of metaphor may also been seen as a way of taking away from the patient the means of participating in his or her own diagnosis and treatment. Unlike specialist jargons, metaphors are part of a common fund, a common knowledge (150–151).

It is clear that the theory of mind-body healing precisely fills the gap Jackson here identifies in biomedicine and makes whole again a process which otherwise remains partial and incomplete.

References

Bradbury, Malcolm
    1987   *Mensonge*. Arrow Books, London.
Cousins, Norman
    1979   *Anatomy of an Illness as Perceived by the Patient*. W. W. Norton,
           New York.
Crapanzano, Vincent
    1980   *Tuhami: Portrait of a Moroccan*. University of Chicago Press,
           Chicago.
d'Aquili, E., C. D. Laughlin, Jr., and J. McManus (editors)
    1979   *The Spectrum of Ritual*. Columbia University Press, New York.
Evans-Pritchard, Edward E.
    1940   *The Nuer*. Clarendon Press, Oxford.
Hymes, Dell (editor)
    1969   *Reinventing Anthropology*. Pantheon, New York.
Jackson, Michael
    1989   *Paths towards a Clearing*. Indiana University Press, Bloomington.
Kirby, V.
    1989   Rewriting: Postmodernism and Ethnography. *Mankind* 19(1):
           36–45.
Le Guin, Ursula K.
    1973   *The Lathe of Heaven*. Avon Books, New York.
    1986   *Always Coming Home*. Bantam Books, New York.
Leach, Edmund
    1961   *Rethinking Anthropology*. Athlone Press, London.
Lock, Margaret, and Nancy Scheper-Hughes
    1987   The Mindful Body: A Prolegomenon to Future Work in Medical
           Anthropology. *Medical Anthropology Quarterly* 1(1):6–41.
Rossi, Ernest L.
    1986   *The Psychobiology of Mind-Body Healing: New Concepts of Therapeutic
           Hypnosis*. W. W. Norton, New York.
Schneider, David M.
    1984   *A Critique of the Concept of Kinship*. University of Chicago Press,
           Chicago.
Smith E., D. Harbour McMenamin, and J. Blalock
    1985   Lymphocyte Production of Endorphins and Endorphin-
           Mediated Immunoregulatory Activity. *Journal of Immunology*
           135(2):779–782.
Strathern, Andrew J.
    1982   Anthropology as Self-Analysis. *Bikmaus* 3(3):93–105.

Turner, Victor
　　1985　*On the Edge of the Bush: Anthropology as Experience*. University of
　　　　Arizona Press, Tuscon.
Tyler, Stephen A.
　　1987　*The Unspeakable: Discourse, Dialogue and Rhetoric in the Post-Modern
　　　　World*. University of Wisconsin Press, Madison.

Conclusion

The main lecture theater at the University of Papua New Guinea was crowded. Its bright lights and the tiers of expectant listeners dazzled and confused me slightly as I entered it. I was keenly aware of the divergent, even contradictory, characteristics of these people, all waiting to see how I could build a bridge between them with the aid of my discipline, anthropology—a discipline already embattled, attacked both by the departing representatives of the colonial power in Papua New Guinea and by the emerging new indigenous elite. Strangely, both sides challenged anthropology as being "useless" to their aims, which they equated with the historical destiny of the country itself. Not long before, ministers of the Australian government had predicted that it would be the year 2000 before the local people could achieve independence, yet self-government in fact came by mid-1974, and full independence came in September 1975. At that crucial point of transition, therefore, what was uppermost in my mind was not so much the viability of one anthropological theory versus another, but the question of whether any kind of anthropology at all could, and should, survive in the new context of Papua New Guinea's emergence as a nation-state. I believed strongly that it should have an enduring place there, for a number of reasons. One was simply that it is a subject of absorbing interest, and Papua New Guinea academics themselves could find delight in it and could make their own developments in it. Another was that its findings, unpalatable as they sometimes were to administrators or politicians, could be used to represent and safeguard the interests of local populations within the new state. Neither reason, however, would necessarily find favor with those in power. Anthropology, as I see it, is an aid to freedom of thought and action, whereas those in power are more often concerned with the control of action. In a sense, therefore, the task which I set for myself in my inaugural lecture, a version of which appears as Chapter 1, was quite simply impossible. Nevertheless, it had to be undertaken, otherwise there could be no justification for taking up a position as professor of Social Anthropology at the University. I chose to tackle the issues by considering what was meant by "tradition" and "development" in discourse current at the time. These terms were employed as rhetorical counters by competing factions within the country to legitimize their own activities and aims and to devalue those of their opponents. The sociologist Joseph Gusfield had pointed this out well before Hobsbawm and Ranger produced their edited collection *The Invention of Tradition* (Hobsbawm and Ranger 1983), and I found his observations particularly well suited for cutting in on the debates about Papua New Guinea's future from the side, as it were. Anthropological perspectives tend to operate by looking at problems from a different angle simply because the placement of the observer is different.

In my case the standpoint was clear. I looked at Papua New Guinea from the level of the local populations outwards. From my knowledge of these populations, particularly in the highlands region, it was clear that the question of tradition versus change was by no means as simple as the development economists and those politicians who listened to them were maintaining. Village people were not so bound by tradition as outsiders believed, since they continuously reshaped their histories in accordance with the contemporary context. In the 1970s modernization theory still held sway, and its application required the belief that village and tribal people were conservative and must be persuaded or pushed into the modern world. It was worthwhile, therefore, to oppose this viewpoint and to regard both "tradition" and "development" as ideological and political categories rather than as descriptive labels for states of society.

Behind this viewpoint, of course, there stands the ghost of Marxist theory, in which, however, I did not take a very serious interest until I actually left Papua New Guinea and returned to the United Kingdom, where in London at University College I found another challenge to the anthropology I first learned in Cambridge in the 1960s. Neo-Marxists were busy dismantling all the concepts of "bourgeois" anthropology, either to discard them entirely or to refashion them in the image of concepts recently developed in Paris by Meillassoux, Terray, Rey, Godelier, and others.

This second challenge brought to me, if anything, a more profound sense of shock than the earlier contextual confrontation I had experienced in Port Moresby. In the first round, motivated certainly by idealistic values, I had felt sure of the discipline I practiced while unsure of myself as its practitioner. I truly felt— as I still do—that the anthropology I know had something valuable to offer to a new nation such as Papua New Guinea, and I was determined to nurture it as a discipline during the transitional period from colonial rule to independence. I was aware, of course, that anthropology itself had been tarred by its alleged association with colonialism, but I fought to liberate it from this association, which I saw as historically contingent rather than necessary and pervasive. Such a belief gave zest to the endless struggle I undertook in Port Moresby to point out the value of anthropological ideas and propositions to those who now grappled with matters of development planning. There were indeed at that time important practical battles to be fought, such as what forms of land tenure should be encouraged for the future. Development planners tended to favor individual tenure on a freehold basis, largely for ethnocentric reasons and for ease of dealing with banks. Historians and anthropologists opposed this view, not in order to obstruct change but to prevent the disastrous effects of abandoning in one stroke the delicate balances achieved in tribal tenure systems between collective and individual claims to resources. The standard technical anthropology of the 1960s was fully adequate in pointing out the falsity of absolute contrasts between communal and individual forms of land tenure and in assessing the ecological effects of different subsistence regimens. The information, in turn, could be presented to politicians and economists at least in the hope of modifying their plans. It was in this sense, then, that I remained convinced of the value of the discipline as such during my five years at that university.

My reaction to the intellectual milieu in London was therefore mixed. The situation was ironic, in my view. Neo-Marxist

anthropologists clearly intended a strong criticism of the exploit-
ative features of world capitalism and, therefore, implicitly also
some kind of a defense of the tribal cultures being undermined by
capitalism. And I, too, had seen myself as in the business of defending tribal cultures. But I did it with the tools fashioned for me
by my anthropological predecessors. In London the neo-Marxists
told me to put all those tools away and develop a new anthropology entirely out of Marxist concepts. They also tended to show a
dislike for what they called purely "empiricist" or, worse, "eclectic" approaches, ones not properly grounded in the revealed
truths of Marxist theory. Many would protest that this is a caricature of their position; but I would reply that even if it is literally a
caricature it nevertheless reveals the rhetorical-ideological spirit
with which they viewed any work that did not sit nicely with their
own categories and concerns. At the same time they appeared to
be more concerned with theoretical categories than with practical
affairs. They were not particularly interested in the fact that I had
actually been in Papua New Guinea for five years at the very heart
of such contradictions and struggles that surround the birth of a
new nation in the Third World. One even shook his head after I
delivered a seminar in which I explained my concern with social
change and asked in apparently genuine (but possibly artful) puzzlement *why* I was studying change. It apparently had not occurred to him that even if I was not studying change in order to
support Marxist—or any—theory at the time, the events were still
of great practical moment to the peoples whose lives I discussed,
and any insights into the processes and trends involved were
therefore worthwhile in themselves. The colleague involved was
at the forefront of the new wave of Marxist thinking, and to this
day he is both scholarly and moderate in his own writings. Yet I
still remember the bitterness of realizing that I could no more convey my enthusiasm and concern for the people in Papua New
Guinea to this colleague than I could to an Australian businessman
concerned only with selling his products there. The businessman
cared only to peddle his wares; and the colleague, it seemed, was
equally concerned only with the propagation of his theories. I continued to view things from "New Guinea outwards" and felt that
metropolitan anthropology partook in a peculiar way of the ideol-

ogy of center-periphery relations which the neo-Marxist project was, in another sense, dedicated to expose. Hence the irony.

A major purpose I had in taking up the chair in Social Anthropology at the University of Papua New Guinea in 1973 was to plant an understanding and appreciation of the subject in a generation of students from whom the country's leaders would undoubtedly be drawn in postindependence times. A further irony I had to deal with then and subsequently was the tendency of some academics to cut the ground away from under their own feet; or sometimes, more conveniently, to steal someone else's ground in order to stand on it by decrying the social sciences as inherently imperialistic and ethnocentric and therefore unsuitable for the Third World countries. This line of thought came out of Africa and, by historical chance, was conveyed to Papua New Guinea through the entry of prominent African academics into the world academic market in the 1960s and 1970s—an entry which was itself a product of the colonial structure of African universities, since they had initially been tied directly to the British university system and had maintained its standards. African academics in Papua New Guinea were not slow to establish an intellectual co-identity with the local people nor, in particular, to press for sociology to be taught *rather than* anthropology. My own view is that this was an unnecessary imposition, no less imperialistic in its way than was the unconscious colonialism of earlier anthropologists. I argued that labels were less important than contents and that the true content of anthropology for Papua New Guinea was to impart an understanding and respect for indigenous cultures not as static entities opposed to the modern world, but as evolving organs of adaptation to an everchanging environment. In order to become an instrument of education in postindependence times, anthropology itself needed to be updated, but not by turning it into sociology, as some of my colleagues at the university appeared to demand. The arrival of sociologist Raymond Apthorpe as an official evaluator of the department's program therefore set off a rather combative phase of relationships. Apthorpe's major sponsor in the department stressed general sociology and methodologies of quantitative research far more than the intricacies of local ethnography. There should have been, as I thought, adequate room for both perspectives; but, as always happens in these matters, one side became evangelistic, and Apthorpe was to be the legitimizing force behind the abolition of anthropology as such in the university and its replacement with "development studies." I saw this as a trap, baited with modernism as a social theory. I felt that it did injustice to the local cultures and was a part of an imposed drive to produce stereotyped patterns of change in the wider society. Apthorpe's report predictably divided the department and caused more conflict than productive change. Chapter 1 has to be seen also, therefore, as my anticipated reply to criticisms that actually did emerge during the Apthorpe visit and my presentation of a counterphilosophy, in which it is the term "development" and not the term "anthropology" that is problematized.

The struggle was by no means over, however, with the departure of Apthorpe, who came and went as consultants tend to do. After my own departure from UPNG for London in 1976, there came to the campus an overseas anthropologist who dedicated himself to a vituperative attack on whatever parts of the anthropology program at the university still stood in place. Returning on a field visit in the late 1970s, I was astonished to hear the contemptuous and dismissive way in which he referred, along with his colleagues, to all aspects of anthropology. However, in an effort to secure a reappointment for himself as a visiting professor for a second year in the department, he was said to have sent a letter to the vice chancellor demanding that this be effected and declaring the support of many prominent student leaders. Unfortunately he had apparently omitted to tell several of these leaders that he was doing this, and when they found out, they opposed him. Even neo-Marxist credentials cannot dispense with a need for democratic action—especially in the turbulent and competitive world of New Guinea micropolitics, whether these be played out in a *haus tamberan* in the Sepik, a men's house in the Highlands, or the main forum of the University of Papua New Guinea. Ironically, then, those who declared themselves to speak for the people sometimes forgot to ask the people first what they should say on their behalf.

The project which topped my own list, and which eventually drew me back to Papua New Guinea from London was the plan to make an Institute of Papua New Guinea Studies (IPNGS) to pursue cultural research not just as an academic subject but integrally with the arts and to produce documents of interest for the Papua New Guinea public. The Institute was largely the brainchild of Ulli and Georgina Beier, who had come a few years earlier from Nigeria to the English department. Ulli, besides being a gifted ethnographer of Yoruba culture, had a remarkable skill for discovering and encouraging literary talent. Georgina was an "artist's artist" with many practical skills as well as her own neat abstract inspiration, and like Ulli she could encourage others. For example, she was midwife to the artistic genius of Kauage, an ordinary, uneducated man from Simbu whose vivid and playful work adorns many an official building and private wall in Papua New Guinea today. These two people, befriended by the then–chief minister, Michael Somare, secured a portion of the five million dollar Australian grant for "culture," given just before Papua New Guinea's independence, and with it set up the Institute in a house in the suburb of Boroko, deliberately away from the university campus.

The new Institute was designed specifically to counterbalance the already existing Institute for Applied Social and Economic Research (IASER), which was an updated version of the New Guinea Research Unit maintained in Port Moresby in colonial times (since the early 1960s) by the Australian National University. The ANU had handed this Unit over to the new Papua New Guinea government and made it available to carry out applied social and economic research, a project from which cultural studies were virtually excluded. A combination of two institutes therefore seemed ideal, and under the genius of the Beiers everything flourished. The IPNGS had small departments devoted to oral history, literature, ethnomusicology, ethnology, and ethnographic film-making, and notable works appeared from all of these, especially in Ulli Beier's field of literature, including a series of novels and poems by John Kolia. The IPNGS had also secured the right to process all applications from foreign research workers to study in Papua New Guinea and to charge a small fee for this service as a means of raising revenue.

Until his departure to return to Africa and thence to settle in Australia in 1979, Beier acted as a one-man band; he orchestrated every activity in the IPNGS for maximum output, but did so without setting up an effective structure that could be operated in his absence. His acting successor, John Kolia, carried this tradition of improvisation further. When I took over the directorship of the Institute in mid-1981, it was already too difficult to halt the trend. We had to fight each year for our budget appropriation, which was always deficient in some crucial regard, including my own salary in the first year I was there! (The struggle I had to secure a reasonable house in which to live would be an instructive example of how already in 1981 it was necessary to use every important connection one had in the public service in order to secure what should have been an automatic right. But it is too long to recount here. Suffice it to say that in the end it came down to the fact that I knew the secretary of Housing and Urban Development from the time he had been the district commissioner in Mount Hagen.) My idea had been to expand the ethnology section of the Institute and obtain within it training fellowships for Papua New Guinean university graduates. I also proposed a National Research Council, which would set policy guidelines for research in the whole country by which the IPNGS could operate. Neither idea came to fruition. The first failed for lack of government money; the second for lack of interest at higher levels in the political system. Politicians just could not be bothered with the concept of such a policy-making body, and the IPNGS had to continue to operate under the provisions of the National Cultural Council.

It was these same provisions, however, that we had to rely upon in order to retain the one formal function of the Institute which still to this day gives it a position of some significance—that is, the right to process, evaluate, and make recommendations regarding research applications which Beier had specifically sought for it as opposed to IASER, recognizing that only so could certain types of research still be encouraged. When I arrived back in 1981, the country's cabinet, the National Executive Council (NEC), had already made a resolution that in principle this power should be removed and given to IASER, which even then was setting up a section to effect the transfer. However, one matter had been overlooked: the NEC's ruling could not be put into effect until the Cultural Act of 1974 was altered, and this had never been done.

Our culture minister at the time, the Honorable Steven Tago, therefore issued a ruling that the research files were national cultural property belonging to his ministry and could not be physically removed. This kept them with the IPNGS, and over time the idea of transferring them was dropped. IASER's hegemony was not established until much more recently, when the IPNGS was incorporated into the National Research Institute, whose central bureaucracy operates from the IASER building in Waigani.

I found myself falling into the Beier pattern of a factotum and involved myself enthusiastically in the work of every section of the IPNGS: in oral history by editing the journal of that name; in literature by contributing to the journal *Bikmaus* (see Chapter 2) and by acting as a judge in folklore in the annual literature competition; in music through collecting trips in the Western and Southern Highlands along with Don Niles; in ethnology by textual transcriptions and translations, including an autobiography by a friend of mine, Ru, to be published by the National Research Institute; and in filmmaking by extensive work in 1983–84 on a spirit cult performance carried out at Kuk in the Western Highlands.

It was undoubtedly this concentration on research, and particularly its Highlands focus, that eventually drew the unfavorable attentions of the National Cultural Council (NCC) from which the directors of National Institutions had earlier been removed. I headed a research institute but had scarcely anyone within it to train; hence, I carried out extensive research myself. I had prolonged my stay at the IPNGS primarily in order to do this, and in the meantime I had been required to give up my tenured position as head of the department and university professor of Anthropology at University College London, in favor of a few open-ended years and no security at the IPNGS. This did not apparently move the NCC, even though the situation was made clear at the time and I explained what I was giving up to stay at IPNGS. My contract went through to mid-1986 and after that was not renewed, despite valiant efforts on my behalf by many good Papua New Guinean friends. The final ironies closed in. I took my chances and visited the Research Group for the Study of Human Ethology in the Max-Planck Institut in Germany, by kind invitation of its leader, Professor I. Eibl-Eibesfeldt, in 1985 and 1986. I also visited Japan, under the terms of a Japan Foundation Fellowship obtained with the assistance of Prof. Sachiko Hatanaka and the Japanese ambassador to Papua New Guinea. Early in 1986 I was invited for a week-long set of interviews for the Andrew W. Mellon Professorship in Anthropology at the University of Pittsburgh, and the letter of appointment was issued, on a visiting basis, before I left the United States. Having departed from academia only a few years earlier to pursue some high ideals and a few personal goals, I landed up back in academia, but in a completely different milieu. At an age when most people's careers are set firmly in a pattern, mine was just beginning again.

Since coming to America, I have opened my mind once more to theoretical issues and trends in anthropology and this is probably made clear in the later chapters of this book. A theme which appears again and again is the tendency to factionalize viewpoints within the subject as a whole; a viewpoint which I have consistently opposed throughout my career from the early 1970s onwards. One of the valuable aspects of so-called postmodernist approaches in anthropology today is their explicit tolerance, even advocacy, of a plurality of intellectual positions and frameworks. Yet there are those within postmodernism who would also wish to refactionalize pluralism by excluding "scientific" ideas altogether. This appears to me unjustified. I end the book, therefore, with some remarks on how I see the field of debate, littered as it is with the dead bodies of false stereotypes and the confusion left over from the battles that rage.

False Dichotomies and "Epistemic Murk"

The breaking down of false stereotypes, often expressed as dichotomies, is one of the most important tasks of anthropology. Today anthropology has most of all to perform this operation on itself, otherwise its progress overall will be impeded. The three stereotypes involved are in principle separate, but in practice they intertwine themselves into a conceptual scheme that divides us along the lines of: interpretation versus explanation, humanism versus science, and culture versus biology. In each case, while we can attribute some sense to the contrast made, it is self-stultifying to allow ourselves to be trapped by it. This is so even more with respect to the total set. If we line ourselves up exclusively on one side or the other we prevent ourselves from utilizing ideas that can lead to a genuine intellectual synergy. Yet this is precisely what schools of thought tend to do. In opening one window, they close another, deliberately or unconsciously. The literature on this topic is large, of course, and has recently come again to the fore through the polarizing work of postmodernist anthropologists on the one hand and sociobiologists on the other. No better totemic examples of what Radcliffe-Brown called "idiographic" versus "nomothetic" forms of inquiry could possibly be found. And one reason why the debates generate more heat than light is that these discussions are not, after all, purely academic. If sociobiologists, for example, appear to give credence to the notion that women's subjugation not only is, but must be, universal, feminists have been prepared passionately to argue against any such "necessity" and have turned to Marxism as their obvious ally in this respect. Over time it has more often been the "scientists" who have trumpeted their views, forcing the "humanists" into retreat—until a "prophet" such as Stephen Tyler arises preaching rather nakedly in the wilderness of his text and announces that science itself, as a historical and cultural artifact, is out-of-date and dead. Books of entirely different persuasion continue to appear, and rather than tackle the whole spectrum I would like to illustrate the contradictions involved by a fairly close inspection of the strengths and weaknesses of two works, which both gain and lose by their intellectual alignment with opposed sides in the "great game." These two books are Paul Stoller's *The Taste of Ethnographic Things* (1989) and Robin Fox's *The Search for Society: Quest for a Biosocial Science and Morality* (1989).

Stoller's book is the outcome of many factors: first, his long-term field research in Africa, with its overtones of personal commitment, attachment, and partial conversion to the people's culture; second, his espousal of postmodern subjectivity, a stance that is connected with his lengthy immersion in the Songhay culture; third, and again related but not logically predictable, is his insistence on the multidimensionality of experience through sound, sight, smell, and taste, hence the title of his book. We meet in his work, therefore, a plea for the anthropologist as person, not just as anonymous scientist, and this at a time in anthropological theorizing when the cross-cultural versions of personhood have themselves increasingly became a focus of attention. The last factor—insistence on the senses—is Stoller's most vital and engaging contribution, the point at which his own individuality is most compellingly presented and a tip or clue toward the construction of an aesthetics of the field experience. Most likely to be contested, on the other hand, is his advocacy for fully adopting the local cultural viewpoint, as in his description of the experiences he encountered during his own apprenticeship in Songhay sorcery.

The text of this book has made much use of the contrast between emic and etic approaches to description and analysis, using these two labels to signify the distinctive epistemological break between actor and observer. Obviously this dichotomy oversimplifies matters. The break is neither absolute nor in all instances clear. Many interstitial positions exist. Conventionally we recognize also that ethnography must be a blend of the emic and the etic; it must give a feel of the view from inside the culture and at least a touch of analysis from outside it. The dichotomous views of practitioners in anthropology, however, tend to cluster around these two labels, turning them into polar opposites. Extreme emics appear to head us deeper and deeper into individual ethnography, thus making it in principle harder to extricate ourselves and scramble back up to the comparative level. Extreme etics, by contrast, reduce all particulars to the universal categories which various brands of philosophy or theory suggest and thereby disregard what is special to any one culture, destroying its "genius" in the name of science. Emics/etics thus comes to be homologous with humanism/science and with relativism/antirelativism. The more anthropologists ensconce themselves within their fieldwork and ethnography, the more they tend inevitably to this version of the emic pole; while the further anthropologists distance themselves, the more likely they are to move towards embracing some version of "grand theory." Robin Fox and Paul Stoller stand as prime examples of these tendencies, Fox on the side of etics and Stoller firmly for emics. Either approach leads to difficulties, however.

Fox's work is based on theories arising out of human ethology and in particular sociobiology. He emphasizes above all the biological character of human sociality and institutions and seeks to impute to these evolutionary functions and mechanisms that have caused them. This is not to say that Fox obliterates the distinction between humans and other animals. By stressing that many forms of behavior are facultative and by granting flexibility to humans, sociobiologists nowadays also generally manage to avoid such a gross error. Instead they are concerned with establishing what constitutes humans as a particular species and therefore, how their cultures will always reflect these species-particular characteristics. In chapter 6 of *The Search for Society*, for example, Fox takes up the question of violence in human social affairs, noting from the start that this is perceived as a "problem" only by humans because of their propensity to seek out and attach meaning to action. Fox finds our tendency to make violence a problem itself rather problematic in the light of natural selection (here destroying the boundary he has at first recognized between humans and other creatures). Since we evolved to kill for food, it continues to be right for us to do so (127). Right, too, that we are altruistic to kin and aggressive to strangers. Violence is made into a problem, Fox argues, by further alterations in society away from its primeval forms in which all was clearly related to reproductive success. Fox concludes that "it is because we are cut off from the roots of violence . . . that we make these things into problems" (131), and this separation has occurred following a social evolution which Fox is forced to agree produces difficulties for us since our own tendencies issue in unintended and undesirable results.

The problem, therefore, for Fox exists entirely in the unintended context in which violence is now set, for example the possibility that one act of violence could destroy large sections of the whole planet we inhabit. It also results from the propensity to ascribe meaning to action, which he has already mentioned, and here his discussion takes on a twist, by means of which he moves from the general to the particular: "The human imagination can take violence in all its natural aspects and . . . create from it elaborate systems of understanding" (1989:135)—out of which in turn come individual wars, battles, and genocide. Thus the problem is not violence but our violent imagination, the same imagination that presumably has created particular cultural systems of meaning as a whole, whether in the sphere of violence or not. Fox is also forced to admit that his own epistemic framework creates a problem here. According to him, nothing we do can be really outside "our nature." So this imagination we have must also be given in this way, and hence it is our nature that has produced the problem for us after all. Back in primeval times, Fox opines, there were no problems of the present kind; the violent activity of males in fact may even have helped to improve their genetic stock through "intelligence, strength, and all-round ability" (141). But now we have created conditions which threaten us, and we have also devised cultures in which violence is actually deplored or suppressed. We have in general made rules and regulations enacted in symbolic nonverbal and verbal codes which hedge our nature with guidelines. Fox argues that these rules also are a product of nature, though it is not entirely clear how this is supposed to have come about. He appeals to the idea that animals also "ritualize" their behavior and hence show us the evolutionary roots of our own. He sees in this, too, a ray of hope for the future, whereby ritualization would replace combat, at least in cases where material interests are not too crucially at stake. The whole argument is intriguing, but its weakest part is precisely where it attempts to turn, as I have noted, from the general to the particular. If our nature is so plastic and our imagination so strong that we can create endlessly variant versions of cultural forms, does not this defeat the project of explaining these forms in the universal terms of ethology or sociobiology? And why should this kind of imagination, this variability, or indeed this strange social evolution, have occurred at all? The mechanisms whereby it happened are not at once given in that "nature" of which Fox is so certain; and should they be perilously dissolved into the specificities of history and culture, science seems to be undone and we are left again with all the problems of cultural anthropology as we know it from our lecture classes and our struggles to write coherent ethnographies.

Whichever way the argument is taken, problems arise about this matter of violence. If it is a result of our naturally developed violent imagination, nature is to blame after all, a conclusion Fox would gladly extricate himself from if he could safely do so. If, on the other hand, imagination is now seen as the unexplained *deus ex machina* which has spawned the individuality of so many diverse cultural systems ("pseudo-speciation," in Eibl-Eibesfeldt's phrase), the peculiarity and indeed diversity of these systems have to be found within and among themselves not by reference to the guiding principles of any "nature," from which they are indeed now alienated. This attempt to encompass emics by etics, or culture by nature, lands us either into blaming nature for our troubles or admitting that the enterprise has broken down because imagination has created forms that are beyond nature. How, then, do we find our way out of this impasse? Paul Stoller, while not directly broaching these problems, would advise us to steer clear of such theory and proceed down a track that he finally labels (echoing—or preceding—the formulation by Michael Jackson) "radical empiricism." In practice this means "ethnography forever."

Stoller's writings, like Fox's, are stimulating, challenging, and extremist. In *The Taste of Ethnographic Things*, Stoller attempts to turn around our thinking and writing in ethnography away from our pseudo-theoretical formulations and jargon and into an appreciation and representation of the sensual forms and meanings created by different cultures. He is the "passionate ethnographer" who describes his pilgrimage over the years in search of knowledge as the Songhay people of Niger conceptualize it. His is also "warts and all" ethnography that reveals much of the conditions of its own production. In positing a Songhay emics, however, Stoller diverges from the postmodernist view that nothing is certain. For him there definitely is a reality out there, and it is a Songhay reality that may take the ethnographer years to come to grips with and experience, but is certainly not ultimately to be questioned. His stance is thus revelatory: truth was revealed to him over time, and he uses vivid writing to convey this truth about the "other," immersing himself in its particularity and its complex details. Songhay culture is alpha and omega to the anthropological vision. Each one of us is thus counseled to go forth and do the same in the cultures we ourselves study.

There is a great deal that is worthwhile in this argument. At a very straightforward level Stoller's complaint against turgid, sometimes indeed shoddy, prose is well taken. Professionalism mystifies; anthropologists create codes that defy rather than produce communication. Yes, certainly, but on the back of this very strong empirical point Stoller has mounted a weaker epistemological one. His ambition here is to question the whole basis of Western-oriented science and philosophy which he sees as going back to Plato and which has produced what the radical philosopher Richard Rorty has dubbed the image of "Our Glassy Essence" (Stoller 1989:146). Rorty suggests that instead of an essentializing philosophy founded on an objective concept of Truth we adopt an edifying philosophy which "is also a kind of pragmatic philosophy that seeks practical solidarity in a living community rather than rarefied objectivity in a mechanistic system" (1989:147). As Stoller himself at once notes, the effect of this is rather bleak in fact: Rorty's "detours" lead us to a place where "conversation has replaced Truth" (148)—in short, to a full-blown postmodernist mystery.

As I have implied, such a conclusion sits uneasily with Stoller's own conviction that there is at least a worthwhile project involved in spending half a lifetime to grasp truth as the Songhay perceive it. If there is a Songhay world, and it can be described, then truth does exist on that ethnographic plane. But truth for the neighboring people will be different; hence, at the intercultural level conversation certainly does replace truth. Truth is relative and culture bound. However, Rorty's deconstructive philosophy in fact undermines even this position, since there is no guarantee that we can ever arrive at anything more than a purely subjective account of "ethnographic things" within a given culture, and hence there can be no intracultural truth either. Extreme postmodernism must lead not to the reconstruction of ethnography—an aim that Stoller has in mind—but to its final death. His own vision is one that is much easier to follow than his flirtation with postmodernist notions. Stoller argues, and I strongly agree, that "we need to describe others as people and give them a voice in our discourse. We need to write ethnographies as multilayered texts that communicate to a number of audiences. We need to acknowledge in the text the presence of an ethnographer who engages in dialogue with his or her subjects" (1989:140).

All this can, and should, be done; but it cannot be done if we are too much in the shadow of a version of postmodernism which ultimately may deny that any account can be better than another. And the fault of this postmodernism is surely that it has passed beyond the point of extreme emics, to which Stoller's own journey leads us, into an uncharted unknown. The problem is that extreme emics do not guard us against this further move. The only element that would guard us would be some version of etics, some theory, which Rorty would diagnose as a "glassy essence." Extreme emics, therefore, expose us to the possibility of a vague and solipsistic world, while extreme etics display to us a world that is transparent (or "glassy"), but the image is banal and one-dimensional.

My conclusion is that both extremes are wrong, or at least unattractive, and that the more viable approach to take is precisely that combination of the emic and etic we consciously or unconsciously practice whenever we write ethnography. As Stoller argues, our texts should be multilayered, and one part of this multiplicity must be a recognition as we write of both the peculiarity and the generality of the phenomena we are representing. In what is usually known as "middle-range analysis," we constantly do this, and some of the most creative efforts at synthetic work continue to be conducted in this mode, as, for example, by Geoffrey Samuel in his book *Mind, Body, and Culture* (1990). Samuel gives us a new "modern" (not postmodern) anthropology by attempting seriously to relate the entities that form the title of his book, and he includes in his battery of concepts the "middle-range" idea of "shamanic mechanisms" of creativity, which he sees as important in directing cultural change over time (chap. 9). If we are to find a resolution of the supposed antinomies of biology and culture or the universal and the particular which have been at the root of the distinction between etics and emics, it must be sought in this area. It is not simply that biology is general and culture is specific, but there is an intimate interplay between the two *and* between the components we have rather crudely labeled "mind" and "body" in our cultural past. And it is here also that a new anthropology can help to create categories of thought different from those on which Western culture has in the past rested, without entirely deconstructing the concept of truth itself. Paul Stoller himself appears to be in sympathy with such an aim when he quotes a Songhay proverb: "if there is no ground, where shall I put my foot?" (1991:983).

It is a puzzling—yet perhaps fitting—experience to finish this text seated not in a university office or a library but in a fieldhouse made of woven cane and thatched with sword-grass, serried ranks of forest trees filling the landscape and wind blowing over the valley from the giant Strickland River, which has long been considered a major cultural barrier between the peoples of the Highlands region of Papua New Guinea and the Ok peoples to their west. Puzzling, because it is always hard to think of general arguments when one is immersed in the minutiae of a particular field enquiry. Fitting, because this is surely diagnostic of the anthropological condition. Each day of fieldwork brings with it the struggle to reach and comprehend the most specific and detailed pieces of information that reach our ears; each evening tends to generate a discussion by means of which we seek to relate these pieces to one another and sometimes to other levels of knowledge we have. Fieldwork and the analysis of data are certainly a work of "bricolage," just as Lévi-Strauss pointed out for the indigenous mythologist. But the art of fieldwork and the point of analysis continue to reside in the fact that not all of the pieces are equally significant, and the act of putting them together in a convincing way has to be both logical and at the same time creative. In this sense anthropology is itself ideally a "shamanic mechanism."

References

Fox, Robin
    1989 *The Search for Society: Quest for a Biosocial Science and Morality.* Rutgers University Press, New Brunswick.
Hobsbawm, Eric J., and Terence O. Ranger
    1983 *The Invention of Tradition.* Cambridge University Press, Cambridge.

Rorty, Richard
   1979   *Philosophy and the Mirror of Nature.* Princeton University Press, Princeton.
Samuel, Geoffrey
   1990   *Mind, Body and Culture.* Cambridge University Press, Cambridge.
Stoller, Paul
   1989   *The Taste of Ethnographic Things: The Senses in Anthropology.* University of Pennsylvania Press, Philadelphia.
   1991   Review of *Modernist Anthropology. American Anthropologist* 93(4):982–983.

Index

Kasaipwalova, John, 82
Kauage, 177
Kinship theory: and definition of
kinship, 23–24, 78–79; and the lineage, 55, 62–63; and marriage, 24–
25; Rivers on English kinship, 70;
and sociobiology, 117–125
Kuper, Adam, 9–10, 54
Kurland, Jeffrey, 121, 122

Labby, David, 57–58
Latukefu, Sione, 15
Leach, Edmund, 24, 35–36, 104
Learning: state-dependent, 163
LeGuin, Ursula, 156
Lévi-Strauss, Claude, 46, 58, 72, 87,
105, 188
Lock, Margaret, 139–140, 159

Magical thought: in advertising, 30;
Daribi, 31
Malinowski, Bronislaw, 42–45, 69;
and colonial power, 50; and his
field diary, 44
Marcus, George, 106
Marxist theory: and consumption,
32–33; and kinship, 25; and mis-
recognition, 23; and precapitalist
societies, 25–27, 131; and study of
meaning, 56; at University College
London, 173–175; and Yapese eth-
nography
Mauss, Marcel: in praise of, 72
Mead, Margaret: on Chambri
(Sepik), 81–82; in Samoa, 79–81
Medical anthropology, 139–145
Meggitt, Mervyn, 85
Mekeo, 82–85
Mind/Body ideas, 139–141, 159–166,
187–188
Missions, Christian: Catholic, 61;
Charismatics, 91; Lutheran, 1–2,
29, 61
Moka, 78, 93, 97
Mosko, Mark, 82–85
Mount Hagen (Melpa): concepts of
sickness, 142–143, 164–165; and

consumption, 34; guns used in
warfare, 135–139; pig killings, 1;
social change, 61; terms for emotions, 89–91
Murdock, George Peter: Huxley lecture, 69–70
Myth: cosmic, in Umeda/Yafar, 86–87

Needham, Rodney, 23–25
Neurobiology, 161
Neuropeptides, 163
Neurotransmitters, 163–164
Noman, 165
Nuer, 54–56

Obeyesekere, Gananath, 111, 116
Ongka, 93

Painkilling drugs: Illich on, 144
Pangia (Wiru), 95
Papau New Guinea, ch. 1 passim;
and anthropology, 171–173; devel-
opment policies in, 12–13; gangs,
137–138; Parliament, 1; University,
3, 7, 175–176
Paradigms: in anthropology, 106–107
Participant observation, 28–29, 43,
67–68; and experience of
feelings, 89
Person, theories of: among Ilongot,
59–60
Phenomenology, 56
Pig-kills, hypothesis regarding, 95
Placebo effect, 162
Politicians (PNG): national: 1–2, 17–
18, 69
Politics, study of, 131–132
Popokl (anger), 90, 165
Popper, Karl, 71
Post-logical mentality, 70
Postmodernism: in work of Paul Stol-
ler, 181, 185–186; and tolerance,
180; in work of Stephen Tyler,
149–150
"Primitive," category of, 6, 15, 84,
129–130